Welcome to *Unique Places in San Francisco*, the premiere edition of Crown Guides. The idea for this book comes from a Dutch series called *Mike's Guides*, published by Made on Earth. We've imported the concept and adapted it to San Francisco, with its alternative culture, easy-going sophistication, and dynamic atmosphere. Crown Guides celebrates small, local specialty establishments—places you won't find anywhere else in the world— and profiles the passionate people behind them. Flip through the pages to find San Francisco treasures you've yet to visit or bring it along on your City outings to help you map out a tour of must-see spots nearby. It was during my own forays throughout San Francisco, mostly on foot, that I discovered the unique and varied places that make up this first Crown Guides volume. The book will be updated each year, and there's also a website—crownguides.com—with links to the websites of featured businesses.

Enjoy all the City has to offer,

Dan Easton
Publisher

Table of Contents

Faerie Queene Chocolate

Confectioner & Tea House

415 Castro Street • San Francisco, CA 94114
415.252.5814 tel • 415.255.2016 fax
www.faeriequeene.com
Castro

HELGA SIGVALDADOTTIR

Open

Tues	11:00-7:00
Wed	11:00-7:00
Thurs	11:00-7:00
Fri	11:00-7:00
Sat	11:00-7:00
Sun	11:00-7:00

5

As if serving gelato and handmade chocolates weren't enough, Faerie Queene recently added an English tea service featuring fresh baked scones and clotted Devonshire cream. Raised in the heart of Dixie, owner Jeoffrey Douglas brings a combination of quick wit, southern charm, and a flair for the dramatic to this tiny jewelbox of a store in the heart of the Castro. Entering the Rococo space feels a bit like stepping into a surreal dreamscape. The ornate interior even shocked one customer into declaring, "This place looks like Barbara Cartland meets Willie Wonka at Victoria's Secret." Douglas's response: Thank you.

Jeoffrey Douglas

MT Home and Body

Home Furnishings & Apparel

4530 18th Street • San Francisco, CA 94114
415.503.0188 tel • 415.621.7605 fax
www.mthomeandbody.com
Castro

Open
Sun   12:00-4:00
And by appointment

HILLARY TURNER

6

Marisa Toriggino

Marisa Toriggino's charming hidden boutique/workshop in the Castro effortlessly combines art and fashion. The peaceful space is filled with luxurious fabrics that are all either hand dyed or hand painted, and most of the work is done on site. The fabrics are then made into throws, pillows, scarves, clothing, tapestries, or detailed paintings. A San Francisco native who traces her roots back to great-grandparents who landed in the Bay Area in the late 19th century, Toriggino studied painting at U.C. Berkeley. Her work has been commissioned for Walt Disney, Paramount Studios, the Guggenheim Museum Store, and is carried at Barneys New York.

home.

Home Furnishings

538 Castro Street • San Francisco, CA 94114
415.824.8585 tel
www.homesanfrancisco.com
Castro

Open

Mon	11:00-9:00
Tues	11:00-9:00
Wed	11:00-9:00
Thurs	11:00-9:00
Fri	11:00-9:00
Sat	10:00-9:00
Sun	11:00-7:00

HELGA SIGVALDADÓTTIR

7

TJ Woodward

Castro District's home is the place to find sculpture with the look and feel of European and Asian antiques at a mere fraction of the cost. That's because every piece is cast here in San Francisco (of a composition of crushed gypsum and cement), and hand-finished. They even do made-to-order pieces, in which you can choose from 12 custom finishes: rustic iron, verdi gris, gold, and wood to name a few. You'll find wall reliefs, columns and pedestals, table bases, urns and candle holders. The rich patina on this statuary might fool even the most discriminating eye, and will add a sense of mystique to *your* home.

Citizen Clothing

Men's Apparel

536 Castro Street • San Francisco, CA 94114
415.558.9429 tel • 415.575.3564 fax
www.bodyclothing.com
Castro

Open

Mon	10:00-8:00
Tues	10:00-8:00
Wed	10:00-8:00
Thurs	10:00-8:00
Fri	10:00-8:00
Sat	10:00-8:00
Sun	11:00-7:00

HELGA SIGVALDADÓTTIR

Petyr

When San Francisco men want to make a fashion statement, they head for Citizen in the heart of the Castro. Here you'll find all the clothing and accessories that make the man—goods from BCBG, DKNY, Calvin Klein, French Connection and Kenneth Cole. London-born Petyr came to the Bay Area for school and decided to make San Francisco his home. His gregarious, friendly nature makes a trip to Citizen more than a shopping spree: It's a social exchange among lovers of fashion and the city. For those occasions when urban attire is not appropriate—at the gym or on the beach—check out BODY, Petyr's other men's clothing store around the corner at 4071 18th Street.

Ver Unica

Vintage Apparel

148 Noe Street • San Francisco, CA 94114
415.431.0688 tel
www.ver-unica.com
Castro

JEREMY BEETON

Open

Mon	12:00-7:00
Tues	12:00-7:00
Wed	12:00-7:00
Thurs	12:00-7:00
Fri	12:00-7:00
Sat	12:00-7:00
Sun	12:00-6:00

9

Amidst the Victorians on tree-lined Noe Street in Duboce Triangle, you'll find Ver Unica. Representing the next wave of recycled fashion, Ver Unica combines impeccably preserved vintage wear from a myriad of eras, along with retro-inspired new items made by local designers. Proprietors Cindy Spade and Willow O'Brien are on hand to share their knowledge and opinions about Ver Unica's clothing selection, and help you cultivate your own unique look.

Cindy & Willow

Atelier 142 Gallery

Art Gallery

2354 Market Street • San Francisco, CA 94114
415.861.8216 tel
www.atelier142.com
Castro

Open
By appointment

JAMES SCOTT GERAS

For all its charms, the Castro has never had a thriving art scene. But all of that changed when classically trained painter Daniel Tousignant and photographer James Scott Geras moved their Haight District gallery/working space to Market and Castro. In addition to showcasing their own work, the duo occasionally features exhibits of other artist's work. Thanks to their efforts, the Castro finally has a fine art gallery. We can only hope they've started a trend.

Daniel Tousignant & James Scott Geras

James Scott Geras

Fine Art Photographer

www.atelier142.com
Castro

Recognized by L.A. Weekly on their list of the top 100 artists of the '90s, photographer James Scott Geras has been published in several major magazines, including Architectural Digest, Cosmopolitan, Elle Decor, People, Vanity Fair, and Vogue. When not shooting for magazines, Geras engages his creative energy in fine art portraits of individuals and couples. Have your portrait done by Geras—for yourself or as a gift for someone special—and you'll see why Arts and Entertainment Magazine declared him, "One of the hottest artists of his generation."

Jungle Red

Hair Salon

4233 18th Street • San Francisco, CA 94114
415.934.9755 tel
Castro

Open
Tues   10:00-7:00
Wed   10:00-7:00
Thurs   10:00-7:00
Fri   10:00-7:00
Sat   9:00-4:30

HELGA SIGVALDADÓTTIR

Swanky. Sexy. Handsome. These are words you'll hear in describing the interior of Jungle Red. With over 20 years experience in hair design, and obvious talent in architectural and interior design, owner Floyd Prewitt created this space to introduce his clients and staff to a lavish yet simple environment. Enthroned in the salon's regal chairs, you'll be pampered under the ministrations of Jungle Red's attentive stylists. Named for the vibrant crimson nail polish that was all the rage in the film classic "The Women," Jungle Red offers great cuts and color, and a custom line of haircare products to maintain your new look.

**Scott, Miko, Mo, Floyd,
Gwen, Andrea & Yvonne**

Bauerware

Cabinet Hardware

3886 17th Street • San Francisco, CA 94114
415.864.3886 tel • 415.864.3889 fax
www.bauerware.com
Castro

Open
Mon   10:00-6:00
Tues   10:00-6:00
Wed   10:00-6:00
Thurs 10:00-6:00
Fri   10:00-6:00
Sat   10:00-6:00

WWW.DAVIDDUNCANLIVINGSTON.COM

13

The sky's the limit at Bauerware Cabinet Hardware. More precisely, the selection of knobs and pulls from over 180 artisans covers the 12-foot walls. Stretch your imagination and select from thousands of possibilities: wood, resin, leather, metal, ceramic, glass, and mahjong tiles. Or you can bring in your own inspired materials and Bauerware will make them cabinet-worthy. Owners Lou Ann Bauer, an award-winning kitchen and bath designer, and Nancy Yost, a "converted" architect, always wanted to own a "different" hardware store, and Bauerware carries their signature quirkiness and playful style. Other people must like it, too. They recently opened a second store in the Willow Glen district of San Jose.

Lou Ann & Nancy

22/23 Restaurant

Restaurant

2223 Market Street • San Francisco, CA 94114
415.431.0692 tel • 415.865.0836 fax
www.2223restaurant.com
Castro

Open

Mon	5:00-10:00
Tues	5:00-10:00
Wed	5:00-10:00
Thurs	5:00-10:00
Fri	5:00-11:00
Sat	11:00-11:00
Sun	11:00-10:00

14

RUDY MYERS

David & Melinda

Even before the no-named restaurant on Market Street adopted its street address as its official moniker, 22/23 Restaurant was already drawing crowds of youthful hipsters and urban acolytes. With its high ceilings, gleaming wood floors, elegant lighting and rotating original art, the atmosphere here is cool and cosmopolitan. But it is chef/owner Melinda Randolph's food that stands out at 22/23—bold, well-orchestrated dishes which seamlessly weave American, Asian, and Mediterranean influences. The seasonal menu is rounded out by sumptuous desserts, an extensive international wine list and innovative specialty cocktails. Under the direction of general manager/owner David Gray, the friendly, professional wait staff is at your service. The good food and festive ambience of one of San Francisco's great neighborhood restaurants make 22/23 a must for the gourmet traveler.

Harvest Ranch Market

Grocer/Deli

2285 Market Street • San Francisco, CA 94114
415.626.0805 tel • 415.626.0905 fax
www.harvestranch.com
Castro

HELGA SIGVALDADÓTTIR

Open

Mon	8:30-11:00
Tues	8:30-11:00
Wed	8:30-11:00
Thurs	8:30-11:00
Fri	8:30-11:00
Sat	8:30-11:00
Sun	8:30-11:00

15

Andrea, Gilles & Carole

Smack in the center of the city at the cusp of several districts is Harvest Market, a grocer/deli that re-defines "neighborhood market." For one thing, Harvest carries fresh food and fine delicacies from over 200 growers, bakeries, dairies, and other food companies throughout the Bay Area. For another, the market has a cozy, inviting ambiance, drawing patrons not only from the surrounding areas but from clear across town. Enjoy their fresh soup-and-salad bar (over 1,000 people do each day) or choose from their outstanding selection of baked goods, prepared foods, and grocery items. The pride of the store is its magnificent produce section, a colorful gallery of farm fresh and organic fruits and vegetables that is as pleasing to look at as to eat. It's easy to see why Harvest is always hopping—its commitment to quality, abundant selection, and urban convenience. Wherever you live, a visit to Harvest Market will convince you to adopt it as your neighborhood market, too.

DESTINO

Restaurant

1815 Market Street • San Francisco, CA 94103
415.552.4451 tel • 415.552.4438 fax
www.destinosf.com
Castro/Upper Market

Open

Mon	5:00-11:00
Tues	5:00-11:00
Wed	5:00-11:00
Thurs	5:00-11:00
Fri	5:00-11:00
Sat	5:00-11:00

16

JAMES SCHENK

Even in restaurant-saturated San Francisco, DESTINO stands out. Centrally situated along Market Street not far from the Mission, the Castro, Hayes Valley and Lower Haight, the Nuevo Latino bistro also straddles culinary boundaries. Former Zuni manager James Schenk offers a unique take on Central and South American cuisine. The menu features tapas and entrees such as empanadas filled with pork loin picadillo and grilled sea bass wrapped in banana leaves. The stellar wine list draws heavily on Argentine and Chilean varietals with Spain and California also making appearances. Fusion desserts like dulce de leche and picarones (Peruvian pumpkin doughnuts) provide a sweet finish. DESTINO's dramatic décor—a beautifully hand-carved wooden door from Peru, dramatic mirrors, mood lighting and a cozy bar—complements the sophistication of the cuisine. The restaurant serves as a tribute to the days when cafes were vehicles; a place to celebrate, dine and relish the joys of life.

James Schenk

Get Lost Travel Books

Bookstore

1825 Market Street • San Francisco, CA 94103
415.437.0529 tel • 415.437.0531 fax
www.getlostbooks.com
Castro/Upper Market

LEE AZUS

Open

Mon	10:00-7:00
Tues	10:00-7:00
Wed	10:00-7:00
Thurs	10:00-7:00
Fri	10:00-7:00
Sat	10:00-6:00
Sun	11:00-5:00

This small, friendly gem of a store specializes in travel. From travel planning to travel kitsch, Get Lost covers the theme. You don't need to bring a Mexican key chain or wind-up walking Michelin man on a trip, but they are typical of the accessories at this unusual store. Of course, you can lose yourself among the 10,000 titles of guidebooks, travel literature, phrase books, atlases, and maps. They sell luggage, electrical adapters, and all the necessary equipment you need for your next trip. And if you just want to dream about travel, there are weekly slide shows and readings on international destinations.

Lee Azus

Kozo Arts

Paper Store

1969A Union Street • San Francisco, CA 94123
415.351.2114 tel • 415.351.1426 fax
www.kozoarts.com
Cow Hollow

Open

Mon	11:00-6:00
Tues	11:00-6:00
Wed	11:00-6:00
Thurs	11:00-6:00
Fri	11:00-6:00
Sat	11:00-7:00
Sun	11:00-6:00

HELGA SIGVALDADÓTTIR

Quality and craftsmanship are the cornerstones of Kozo Arts, a store specializing in handcrafted bookbinding and decorative papers. The talented artisans at this Union Street studio/boutique design and create exquisite photo albums, decorative boxes, journals, picture frames, and desk accessories. In addition, owner Linda Barrett and her staff custom-design products for any occasion or use. The inspiration lies in the materials—handmade textured and silk-screened papers, imported silk brocades, pristine archival pages. Each handmade album and book draws upon centuries-old bookbinding traditions and is an individual work of art. Kozo Arts carries one of the finest lines of paper creations anywhere, and their selection of decorative papers may well inspire you to undertake your own creative projects.

Notara, Michelle, Eriko, Kristin & Linda

ATYS

Contemporary Living Accessories

2149-B Union Street • San Francisco, CA 94123
415.441.9220 tel • 415.643.1050 fax
www.atysdesign.com
Cow Hollow

HELGA SIGVALDADÓTTIR

19

Open

Mon	11:00-6:30
Tues	11:00-6:30
Wed	11:00-6:30
Thurs	11:00-6:30
Fri	11:00-6:30
Sat	11:00-6:30
Sun	11:00-6:30

Paul Kerr

Tucked away in an historic Cow Hollow courtyard, you'll find ATYS (pronounced ah-tees) a design shop catering to those tired of cookie-cutter décor. (That's everyone, right?) Don't be deceived by its hidden location. Within its minimalist architecture, owner Paul Kerr has amassed a selection of eye-catching modern objects and boldly designed home accents from Scandinavia, Italy, Germany, and the United States. Here, beauty is bolstered by innovation, elegance by originality. Trust that your unique selection will spark inquiries among your friends… "Wherever did you find this?" That's worth going out of your way for.

Nneka

Women's Apparel & Wedding Gowns

2278 Union Street • San Francisco, CA 94123
415.931.6541 tel • 415.931.7384 fax
www.nneka.com
Cow Hollow

Open

Mon	11:00-7:00
Tues	11:00-7:00
Wed	11:00-7:00
Thurs	11:00-7:00
Fri	11:00-7:00
Sat	11:00-7:00
Sun	11:00-5:00

20

HELGA SIGVALDADÓTTIR

Penny Adibe

When the revolution finally arrives, what will you be wearing? Designer Penny Adibe has a few ideas. Her boutique, Nneka, features clothing for women that combines elegance and irreverence, formality and fun, satin and pleather. Adibe considers fashion a basic form of expression and her designs are statements of simplicity, directness, and self-confidence. The store's name is Nigerian for "the woman is greater." Thanks to Adibe, she's well-dressed too.

Oceana Rain Apparel

Women's Apparel

3024 Fillmore Street • San Francisco, CA 94123
415.346.2797 tel • 415.346.2330 fax
www.oceanarain.com
Cow Hollow

CESAR RUBIO

Open

Mon	11:00-7:00
Tues	11:00-7:00
Wed	11:00-7:00
Thurs	11:00-7:00
Fri	11:00-7:00
Sat	11:00-7:00
Sun	12:00-6:00

21

Self-expression is all in a day's work at Oceana Rain Apparel. The Cow Hollow/Pacific Heights boutique was started by a former model and fashion designer. These days, Oceana prefers being out of the spotlight, traveling to Italy, France, and England to seek out the latest European designers. She also carries a strong group of American designers, including Diane von Furstenberg, Poleci, Rebecca Taylor, Jil Stuart, and Daryl K., as well as her own label. From irresistible lingerie to comfy lounge wear, from weekend wear to formalwear, there's something for every occasion. Add to that about a dozen styles of shoes and a unique selection of jewelry, and Oceana Rain Apparel is a one-stop boutique.

Oceana Rain

John Wheatman & Associates

Home Furnishings/Interior Designers

1933 Union Street • San Francisco, CA 94123
415.346.8300 tel • 415.771.8652 fax
Cow Hollow

Open

Mon	10:00-5:00
Tues	10:00-5:00
Wed	10:00-5:00
Thurs	10:00-5:00
Fri	10:00-5:00
Sat	10:00-5:00

DAVID WAKELY

Interior designers John Wheatman and Associates have been creating beautiful and highly functional living spaces for 30-plus years. When you visit Wheatman's Union Street Shop—a series of elegant room settings spread over three levels—you will instantly understand the firm's success. Savor the burble of the outdoor fountain in the garden space you pass through on your way to the stairs. Fall in love with the massive tansu, the intriguing metal sculpture, or the exquisite High Wycombe chair in the corner. But don't walk away empty-handed, unless you can live without the object of your desire—chances are good that the piece is a rarity acquired on a foreign buying trip or one of Wheatman's own designs, manufactured exclusively for the firm.

John Wheatman

77 Maiden Lane Salon & Spa

Hair Salon & Spa

77 Maiden Lane, 2nd Floor • San Francisco, CA 94108
415.391.7777 tel • 415.391.0877 fax
www.77maidenlane.citysearch.com
Downtown

MARK DARLEY

Open

Mon	9:00-6:00
Tues	9:00-7:00
Wed	9:00-7:00
Thurs	9:00-8:00
Fri	9:00-7:00
Sat	9:00-6:00
Sun	10:00-6:00

23

Sherlee Rhine

For the ultimate in indulgence, look no further than 77 Maiden Lane. From its beginnings as a salon on tiny Maiden Lane, to its expansion as a day spa, owner Sherlee Rhine's commitment to top-notch service has remained constant. 77 Maiden Lane offers hair design, makeup consultations, facial treatments, body massage, and hand, leg and foot therapy in an elegant setting, allowing you to pamper yourself from head to toe. Whether you desire a relaxing 80-minute massage, Vitamin C facial or daylong spa package, Rhine and her specialists do it all. Hair and makeup styling for weddings are also available—they even make house calls.

kar'ikter

Gift & Children's Store

418 Sutter Street • San Francisco, CA 94108
415.434.1120 tel • 415.434.2691 fax
www.karikter.com
Downtown

Open

Mon	10:00-6:00
Tues	10:00-6:00
Wed	10:00-6:00
Thurs	10:00-6:00
Fri	10:00-6:00
Sat	10:00-6:00
Sun	11:00-5:00

24

SHERIDAN KEITH

Carol, Tintin & Cath

Kar'ikter is the sort of store designed for the child in all of us. It specializes in products based on European comic book characters like the space-traveling Tintin, the urbane Babar, and the winsome, wise Little Prince. In this context, you'll also find colorful contemporary designed-oriented gifts and home accessories imported by owners Cath Morrison and Carol Malcolm from England, France, Denmark, the Netherlands, Italy, and Germany. There are school supplies, books, wristwatches, and tableware interspersed with cheeky Philippe Starck stools, Kartell tables and inventive Alessi home furnishings. (For a more extensive selection of Alessi products, check out the recently opened Alessi shop directly next door at 424 Sutter Street.) Choose the items that make you smile and forget your deadlines.

Cafe de la Presse

Bar, Cafe, Restaurant & International News Stand

352 Grant Avenue • San Francisco, CA 94108
415.398.2680 tel • 415.249.0916 fax
www.cafedelapresse.com
Downtown

Open

Mon	7:00-11:00
Tues	7:00-11:00
Wed	7:00-11:00
Thurs	7:00-11:00
Fri	7:00-11:00
Sat	7:00-11:00
Sun	7:00-11:00

New Orleans is not the only American city that boasts a Quartier Francais. At the heart of a cluster of French cafes and restaurants and near the Consulate and the French Church, Cafe de la Presse reigns as San Francisco's consummate people-watching place, European-style. Featuring a full-service restaurant, cafe with outdoor seating, and international newsstand, Cafe de la Presse plays host each day to more than 1,000 locals and visitors from all over the world. You can enjoy a French meal in the dining room, or their famous croque-monsieur in the café. Put on some dark shades, tuck a pack of Gauloises in your pocket, and murmur your order to the waiter. While you sip your bowl of coffee or glass of vin rouge, catch up on the news in Le Figaro, read Hugo in his language, or simply watch the world go by.

Mr. Gabriel

MAC

Men's & Women's Apparel

5 Claude Lane Street • San Francisco, CA 94108
1543 Grant Avenue • San Francisco, CA 94133
415.837.0615 tel (Downtown) • 415.837.1604 tel (North Beach)
Downtown & North Beach

Open

Mon	11:00-6:00
Tues	11:00-6:00
Wed	11:00-6:00
Thurs	11:00-6:00
Fri	11:00-6:00
Sat	11:00-6:00
Sun	12:00-5:00

26

HELGA SIGVALDADÓTTIR

Ben & Chris

After 20 years in business, MAC's success derives from a focus on up-to-the-minute design, cumulative decades of fashion know-how, and strong family ties. Siblings Ben and Chris Ospital returned to San Francisco with mom Jeri and decided to put their New York fashion experience to work in their hometown. The product of their labor is MAC. These his and hers boutiques share a commitment to free-spirited clothing, innovative designs, and a bohemian sensibility in products from Europe as well as homegrown talents. Women's lines include Dema, Manifesto:, Anna Sui and Miller et Bertaux. Men's lines include John Bartlett, William Reid, Oliver Helden, and Armand Basi. The men's store also carries the latest in home accessories from Droog Design and Ken Wingard among others. MAC is known for getting there first, and they will soon carry Lemon Twist's new line of baby clothes: Lemon Drop. MAC, ever the stylish family-run shop, is now the place where you can shop in style for the whole family.

Utopia Planitia

Women's Apparel

624 Bush Street • San Francisco, CA 94108
415.362.1277 tel
www.uplanitia.com
Downtown

Open

Mon	12:00-6:30
Tues	12:00-6:30
Wed	12:00-6:30
Thurs	12:00-6:30
Fri	11:00-6:30
Sat	11:00-6:30

27

LORI EANES

Few inhabit the "fashion forward" designation as well as design duo Minnie Yeh and Charles Burrows. Their women's clothing boutique, Utopia Planitia, is named for both a crater on Mars and a "Star Trek" space station. With its philosophy of "Modern, Luxe, Style," Utopia Planitia's clothing blends classic silhouettes in natural fibers, with current references and feminine details including beading and embroidery. This San Francisco store features an aluminum and glass storefront, Eames-inspired dimple door and counter, rotating local art, stainless steel fixtures and sandblasted Lucite shelves. An interlocking cubic structure inspired by Zaha Hadid's Cincinnati Museum of Art model displays jewelry. The clothing selection and home line selection are just as exacting, and reflect luxurious, cutting-edge fashion and accessories from around the world.

Charles & Minnie

shine

Women's Shoes & Accessories

808 Sutter Street • San Francisco, CA 94109
415.409.0991 tel • 801.761.6991 fax
shine_online@yahoo.com
Downtown

Open

Tues	11:00-7:00
Wed	11:00-7:00
Thurs	11:00-7:00
Fri	11:00-7:00
Sat	11:00-6:00
Sun	11:00-6:00

28

HEATHER DE KONING

Even though it's only been open since June 2000, shine is already diverting traffic from nearby Union Square with an eclectic mix of women's shoes and accessories from local, national, and international designers. Owner Tristan Cameron, a Washington, D.C. transplant, does the buying for the small but well-stocked Sutter Street store. shine carries more than 25 designers, including Cynthia Rowley, Lisa Nading, Ipa-nima, Stein Blye, and Jules & Jim Paris. Although handbags have emerged as a specialty, shine also carries hair clips and jewelry, and Cameron is constantly on the lookout for new, unusual items. Footwear ranges from sandals and flats to pumps and boots. With its vibrant hues and gamut of styles, shine is a destination in and of itself.

Tristan

Metier

Women's Apparel

355 Sutter Street • San Francisco, CA 94108
415.989.5395 tel • 415.986.7603 fax
metier@sirius.com
Downtown

MATTHEW MILLMAN

Open	
Mon	10:00-6:00
Tues	10:00-6:00
Wed	10:00-6:00
Thurs	10:00-6:00
Fri	10:00-6:00
Sat	10:00-6:00

29

Sheri

Every season, Metier owner Sheri Evans selects the most seductive pieces by designers who share her preference for feminine silhouettes and fresh palettes. Her mixture of the crisp (Katayone Adeli, Daryl K, Chaiken), the diaphanous (Rozae Nichols), the playful (Rebecca Taylor, Development), and the frankly sexy (Anna Molinari's stretchy flowered sweaters and dolce vita dresses, Cosabella lingerie) consistently draws neo-bohemians, creative professionals, and women who simply love beautiful things to the sun-washed store. Other enticements include sorbet-colored hand-knits by Souchi and Ursula Beaugeste handbags in leather and canvas. For further adventures in personal adornment, check out the jewelry case, where contemporary artists—Cathy Waterman's megawatt diamond creations, Jeanine Payer's hand-inscribed silver—share space with Georgian jet earrings and Victorian cuffs. Selected for their staying power, these designs endure as trends ebb and flow.

M²

Hair Salon

912 Sutter Street • San Francisco, CA 94109
1555 California Street • San Francisco, CA 94109
415.474.6262 tel (California Street) • 415.409.6262 tel (Sutter Street)
Downtown

Open

Tues	1:00-7:00
Wed	1:00-7:00
Thurs	1:00-7:00
Fri	1:00-7:00
Sat	10:00-5:00
Sun	12:00-5:00

30

HELGA SIGVALDADÓTTIR

Michael Page

Beauty through simplicity is the philosophy behind M², a hair salon with two central locations. Specializing in cuts and color, the stylists at Michael Page's salons turn out cuts that are dramatic, yet basic, and blend colors that complement rather than clash. Goodbye, dull hair. The spare, elegant space at the new Sutter location sends the message even before you sit in one of Randy Castellon-designed Lucite chairs. You'll emerge from M² transformed and ravishing, your life a series of good-hair days.

Sugar

Home Furnishings

804 Sutter Street • San Francisco, CA 94109
415.409.7842 tel • 415.409.7843 fax
www.sugardecor.com
Downtown

HELGA SIGVALDADÓTTIR

Open

Mon	1:00-7:00
Tues	1:00-7:00
Wed	1:00-7:00
Thurs	1:00-7:00
Fri	1:00-7:00
Sat	1:00-7:00
Sun	1:00-7:00

31

At Sugar, the new home furnishings store on Sutter, less is more. Striking objects and designer furniture adorn a simple white space—minimalism meets installation art. Owner Michael Page carefully selects and arranges the merchandise into life-size dioramas of modern design. Wares include console tables and pedestals by Randy Castellon, pottery by Ceci, lighting by R & D Design, bedding by Dwell, pillows by Jonathan Adler, and hand-painted fire extinguishers by Nuda. Sugar brings gallery aesthetics to domestic design. Sweet.

Michael Page

Britex Fabrics

Fabric Store

146 Geary Street • San Francisco, CA 94108
415.392.2910 tel • 415.392.3906 fax
www.britexfabrics.com
Downtown

Open

Mon	9:30-6:00
Tues	9:30-6:00
Wed	9:30-6:00
Thurs	9:30-7:00
Fri	9:30-7:00
Sat	9:30-6:00

32

KENNETH LEE

**Lucy &
Beverly Spector**

Four floors, 12,000 square feet, countless bolts of fine fabrics, 40,000 different buttons, vast quantities of trims, ribbons, and remnants, 50 employees, open six days a week. This is easy math. After half-century in business, Britex simply offers an unsurpassed selection. Owner Lucy Spector travels to mills in Europe to personally select Britex's quality wares. And you, dear shopper, are the beneficiary of her extensive experience and discerning tastes. Confer with Lucy and her staff in any of 18 languages. They'll help you shape a fashion statement, choose the ideal upholstery, or survive your first sewing project. This is the kind of hands-on experience our grandmothers took for granted; it lives on at Britex.

David Stephen Menswear

Men's Clothing

50 Maiden Lane • San Francisco, CA 94108
415.982.1611 tel • 415.982.0418 fax
www.davidstephen.com
Downtown

DAVID STEPHEN COLLECTION

Open

Mon	9:30-5:30
Tues	9:30-5:30
Wed	9:30-5:30
Thurs	9:30-5:30
Fri	9:30-5:30
Sat	9:30-5:30

And by appointment

33

Like their counterparts in Milan and London, David Stephen Menswear carries on the venerable European tradition of offering exquisite men's clothing and expert tailoring under one roof. Since 1969, this has been the place to indulge your tastes for consummate quality, classic comfort, and fine fabrics—elegant silks, Merino wool, 10-ply cashmere. Sportswear lines includes Zegna, Canali, Zanella, and Incotex. A visit to David Stephen will have you turned out as dapper and debonair as 007 or as smooth and suave as the Sheik. They'll supply the clothes; you'll have to provide the charm.

David Gronowski & Jack Ried

La Maison de la Bouquetière

Home Furnishings

563 Sutter Street • San Francisco, CA 94102
415.248.1120 tel • 415.248.1121 fax
www.labouquetiere.com
Downtown

Open

Mon	10:30-7:00
Tues	10:30-7:00
Wed	10:30-7:00
Thurs	10:30-7:00
Fri	10:30-7:00
Sat	10:30-7:00

34

LA BOUQUETIERE COLLECTION

Though they're known worldwide for their exquisite line of scented candles and bath and body products, their only retail store is right here in San Francisco. La Maison de la Bouquetière, Raul Mario Salas's Sutter Street boutique, is evocative of an elegant French salon. Rooms devoted to dining, bed, bath, and nursery feature beautiful gifts as well as everyday items. Authentic bistro table settings, colored glasswear and dishes, imported cotton children's clothing, chandeliers and furniture finds from flea markets are just a few of the store's offerings. French music plays in the background, and the scent of incense and aromatic candles fill the air.

Bell'occhio

Ribbon & Gift Store

8 Brady Street • San Francisco, CA 94103
415.864.4048 tel • 415.864.2626 fax
www.bellocchio.com
Downtown/Upper Market

CLAUDIA SCHWARTZ

Open

Tues	11:00-5:00
Wed	11:00-5:00
Thurs	11:00-5:00
Fri	11:00-5:00
Sat	11:00-5:00

35

Bell'occhio, which means "beautiful eye" in Italian, has been enchanting its customers with a charming and otherworldly shopping experience for over 12 years. Inspired by the beauty and workmanship of ephemeral and rarefied objects, the store showcases examples of the European métiers, including elegant boxes, antique ribbons, handmade silk flowers, Santa Maria Novella toiletries, Parisian face powders and perfumes, as well as an assortment of curiosities. All these items are displayed with a light and often humorous touch, and nary a parcel leaves the store without the extravagant wrapping for which the store is known. At Bell'occhio, one will encounter an evocative atmosphere that relates seamlessly from its heady scent and its esoteric musical offerings to its attentive staff.

Claudia Schwartz

Modern Artifacts

Furniture & Home Furnishings

1639 Market Street • San Francisco, CA 94102
415.255.9000 tel • 415.255.9000 fax
www.modernartifacts.net
Downtown/Upper Market

Open

Mon	1:00-6:00
Thurs	1:00-6:00
Fri	1:00-6:00
Sat	1:00-6:00
Sun	1:00-6:00

HELGA SIGVALDADÓTTIR

36

Chris & Carole

For the best in current and classic 20th century design, seek out Modern Artifacts. Here, you'll find uniquely designed objects and furniture for home, studio, and office. Designers include Kjaerholm, the Eameses, Florence Knoll, and SFMOMA architect Mario Botta. Owner Chris Houston and assistant Carole Scott have effectively curated a vibrant testament to modern design ingenuity while taking the starch out of high design. With an eye toward the practical and functional, Chris and Carole will help you to visualize a home where museum pieces can get comfortable and you can try on art for size.

New Deal

Furniture & Home Furnishings

1632b Market Street • San Francisco, CA 94102
415.552.6208 tel • 415.552.6208 fax
www.newdealhome.com
Downtown/Upper Market

ALBERT DOWNS

Open

Mon	11:00-7:00
Wed	11:00-7:00
Thurs	11:00-7:00
Fri	11:00-7:00
Sat	11:00-5:00
Sun	11:00-5:00

37

Back in 1993, at the height of the economic recession, long-time friends and designers Terje Arnesen and Albert Downs risked their savings on a furniture and home furnishings business they dubbed a "city store." They envisioned a selection of eclectic furniture and accents designed for urban ease and aesthetic pleasure. The fruit of their labor is New Deal, a showroom crammed with versatile decor for San Francisco spaces (which aren't always spacious). Here, Mission-style practicality meets Danish elegance with flourishes of '50s chic. For the walls, New Deal offers San Francisco cityscapes by painter Sergio Galli. What better way to make your tiny studio seem bigger than by bringing California Street inside?

Terje Arnesen

Albert Downs

Decodence

Furniture & Home Furnishings

1684 Market Street • San Francisco, CA 94102
415.553.4525 tel • 415.553.4521 fax
www.decodence.com
Downtown/Upper Market

Open

Wed	11:00-6:00
Thurs	11:00-6:00
Fri	11:00-6:00
Sat	11:00-6:00
Sun	12:00-5:00

And by appointment

38

PETER LINDEN

The wrought-iron Deco gates are the first indication of where you are—Decodence, a store specializing in 20th century objects. Here you'll find the simple symmetries of Art Deco and the elaborate flourishes of Art Nouveau side by side. Owners Peter Linden and Eric Menard started as collectors and were later joined by Peter's sister, Tina Whelon. The selection at Decodence owes much to their accumulated wisdom and eye for detail. These pristine design artifacts include original furniture by designers such as Deskey, Rohde, and Frankl as well as French glassware from René Lalique, Charles Schneider, and Daum Nancy. Peruse their selection of more than 15,000 objects. You're bound to find a piece of the 20th century just right for your 21st century home.

Peter Linden, Eric Menard & Tina Whelon

Nest

Home Furnishings

2300 Fillmore Street • San Francisco, CA 94115
2340 Polk Street • San Francisco, CA 94109
415.292.6199 tel (Fillmore) • 415.292.6198 tel (Russian Hill)
Fillmore & Russian Hill

HELGA SIGVALDADÓTTIR

Open

Mon	10:30-6:30
Tue	10:30-6:30
Wed	10:30-6:30
Thurs	10:30-6:30
Fri	10:30-6:30
Sat	10:30-6:30
Sun	12:00-6:00

39

Mother-and-daughter team Judith Gilman and Marcella Madsen have been frequenting French fleas markets since Marcella was just a baby. Now they've poured all that valuable shopping experience into Nest, a Parisian-style boutique located in a former pharmacy on Fillmore. The old apothecary cabinets offer a fitting backdrop to the one-of-a-kind furnishings and distinctive housewares culled from ateliers and small manufactures throughout France and England: glassware, linens, toiletries, teas. The displays speak of history and rustic elegance, all arranged in a cozy, warm space. Just look for the sign bearing a nest. Then settle in to shop. And beginning in May 2001, you can visit their second store at 2340 Polk Street.

Judy Gilman & Marcella Madsen

Paolo

Men's and Women's Shoes

1971 Sutter Street • San Francisco, CA 94115
415.885.5701 tel • 415.885.5702 fax
www.paoloshoes.com
Fillmore

Open

Mon	11:00-7:00
Tues	11:00-7:00
Wed	11:00-7:00
Thurs	11:00-7:00
Fri	11:00-7:00
Sat	11:00-7:00
Sun	12:00-6:00

40

HELGA SIGVALDADÓTTIR

Paolo Iantorno

At Paolo, the relationship between the shoe and the foot is so intimate it's considered a marriage. Owner Paolo Iantorno, who grew up in San Francisco and Italy, visits factories in Italy and has them produce the coolest designs for his Pacific Heights boutique. Iantorno designs two collections a year, with 160 styles for men and women in each. All styles are produced in over 30 different factories across Northern Italy. Leathers and textiles are hand selected, and each shoe is inspected throughout the production process to ensure the highest product quality available. The handmade workmanship, focus on color and unusual heels will make Gucci and Prada fans feel right at home. The store is designed to resemble a Roman piazza. Weathered fountains, vases, and sculptures complete the old-Italy effect.

George

Pet Store

2411 California Street • San Francisco, CA 94115
415.441.0564 tel • 415.441.4644 fax
www.georgesf.com
Fillmore

KAREN STEFFENS

Open	
Mon	11:00-6:00
Tues	11:00-6:00
Wed	11:00-6:00
Thurs	11:00-6:00
Fri	11:00-6:00
Sat	10:00-6:00
Sun	12:00-6:00

Ten years ago, two design-conscious pet owners set out to make products that were as pleasing to people as they were to their pets. With a (now) 14-year old Fox Terrier named George as inspiration and focus group, the three went to work. Today, two George stores offer cool cats, canines, and their grateful owners styling accessories to wear, chase, eat, and play with. Featured in magazines such as Metropolitan Home, House & Garden, and In Style, the George collection includes everything from "Good Dog" bath towels to the "Cat Trip" velveteen catnip toys, tartan plaid collars, baked-from-scratch treats, natty jackets, lucky charms, laurel wreath chew toys, vintage ticking beds, corduroy quilts, ceramic bowls, nifty carrying cases, enamel ID tags, and an ever-changing array of T-shirts, sweatshirts, and caps for bipeds.

Bobby Wise & George

Max Furniture

Furniture

1633 Fillmore Street • San Francisco, CA 94115
415.440.9002 tel • 415.440.9003 fax
www.maxdsn.com
Fillmore

Open

Tues	11:00-7:00
Wed	11:00-7:00
Thurs	11:00-7:00
Fri	11:00-7:00
Sat	11:00-7:00
Sun	12:00-5:00

MARGOT CRISCITIELLO

James Do

Vietnamese-born designer James Do started MAX Furniture back in 1990, selling his versatile line to retailers, architects, and designers. Now, with its spacious showroom on Fillmore, MAX Furniture is celebrating its first year offering Do's graceful, modern, functional pieces directly to the public. With a background in art, engineering, and architecture, Do incorporates a range of design influences in his work—Japanese simplicity, French elegance, American utility. His cabinets, bookcases, and tables display superior workmanship, and his materials include striking combinations of lustrous woods, brushed steel accents, and frosted glass panels. Happily, the dimensions and materials of most pieces can be modified to meet your specific needs, since you'll likely find something that would really pull your living room together. If you need more help, fear not. MAX Furniture also provides interior design services.

Big Pagoda Company

Home Furnishings & Art Gallery

1903 Fillmore Street • San Francisco, CA 94115
415.563.8727 tel • 415.563.8726 fax
www.bigpagoda.com
Fillmore

IAN REEVES

Open

Tues	11:00-7:00
Wed	11:00-7:00
Thurs	11:00-7:00
Fri	11:00-7:00
Sat	11:00-7:00
Sun	12:00-6:00

43

Kurt Silver

You will be surrounded by harmony, grace, and light. So might read your fortune before entering Big Pagoda Company, a home furnishings store and art gallery dedicated to the blissful marriage of seemingly opposing design impulses— classic and contemporary, elegance and irreverence, East and West. Proprietor Kurt Silver opened Big Pagoda following a 10-year sojourn in Asia and its mix of influences is shaped by his finely-honed appreciation of beauty. The store itself is spacious and pleasing, providing a perfect venue for the authentic antiques, classic reproductions, contemporary designs, and provocative art arranged in accordance with its own signature aesthetic, "funk shui." Says Silver: "We just try not to be dull."

Zinc Details

Home Furnishings

1905 Fillmore Street • San Francisco, CA 94115
415.776.2100 tel • 415.776.2232 fax
www.zincdetails.com
Fillmore

Open

Mon	11:00-7:00
Tues	11:00-7:00
Wed	11:00-7:00
Thurs	11:00-7:00
Fri	11:00-7:00
Sat	11:00-7:00
Sun	12:00-6:00

44

HELGA SIGVALDADÓTTIR

Vasilio Kiniris

From its beginnings in a tiny downtown space to its current spacious digs in Pacific Heights, Zinc Details has maintained its commitment to functional, durable, and affordable design. The selection of contemporary classics reflects proprietors Vasilio and Wendy Kiniris's philosophy that products should meet customer's everyday needs and inspire simplicity and ease of living. To that end, the store features areas devoted to urban gardens, design, casual living, and the kitchen, linked by an allegiance to Japanese and Scandinavian design and a fireworks display of color. Interspersed amongst the store's collection of International design is Zinc Details own line of dinnerware, lighting, and other contemporary living accessories. The design of the store itself has won Zinc Details awards and recognition in glossies such as Elle Decor, Metropolitan Home, Surface, I.D. Magazine, and House and Garden.

Boulangerie Bay Bread

Boulangerie

2325 Pine Street • San Francisco, CA 94115
2310 Polk Street • San Francisco, CA 94119
415.440.0356 tel (Fillmore) • 415.345.1107 tel (Russian Hill)
Fillmore & Russian Hill

Open: Fillmore

Tues	8:00-6:00
Wed	8:00-6:00
Thurs	8:00-6:00
Fri	8:00-6:00
Sat	8:00-6:00
Sun	8:00-4:00

Open: Russian Hill

Tues	7:00-7:00
Wed	7:00-7:00
Thurs	7:00-7:00
Fri	7:00-7:00
Sat	7:00-7:00
Sun	7:00-7:00

HELGA SIGVALDADÓTTIR

Pascal

Baguette, levain, brioche, Madeleine, croissants, pain au chocolat—the words conjure up a delectable vision of a small bakery one stumbles across on a first trip to France and never forgets. Luckily for San Francisco, Bordeaux native Pascal Rigo decided to share his love of bread and pastries, and with partner Lori Goodman created a rustic French country bakery just off Fillmore Street in 1999. From the organic flour and imported Pavailler ovens to the baskets of crusty breads and the aroma of fresh-baked pastries, Boulangerie is the real thing. Customers know it, and jam into the small shop and line up outside in anticipation of that perfect, buttery concoction they'll soon have in their hands. Recognizing its runaway success, Boulangerie now has a second location on Polk Street.

45

Heather

Women's Apparel

2408 Fillmore Street • San Francisco, CA 94115
415.409.4410 tel • 415.409.4412 fax
Fillmore

Open

Mon	10:30-6:30
Tues	10:30-6:30
Wed	10:30-6:30
Thurs	10:30-6:30
Fri	10:30-6:30
Sat	10:30-6:30
Sun	12:00-5:00

46

HEATHER DE KONING

Bright flowers in window boxes welcome Fillmore Street strollers to this eponymous women's clothing boutique. Heather carries an array of international designers, including England's Allegra Hicks loungewear and John Smedley's knitwear, Japan's Peplum, Spain's Luis Is, France's Herve Chapelier handbags, and America's Blue Dot, New Frontier and Passion Bait. It's a diverse group, but they share beautiful design and high quality: "Things women will love and use over time, not just the latest passing trend," says owner Heather Frazier. In addition to clothing the body, Heather also offers something for the soul, with an ever-changing mix of vintage and contemporary photographs, and books. Aromatherapy body and facial oils complete the experience.

Heather Frazier & Charles Hartman

Annies

Women's Apparel

2512 Sacramento Street • San Francisco, CA 94115
415.292.7164 tel • 415.292.7165 fax
www.anniesclothing.com
Fillmore

JENNIFER PADGETT

Open

Mon	11:00-7:00
Tues	11:00-7:00
Wed	11:00-7:00
Thurs	11:00-7:00
Fri	11:00-7:00
Sat	11:00-7:00
Sun	11:00-5:00

47

Nestled on a side street in tony Pacific Heights lies Annies, the destination boutique for San Francisco hipsters. Style mavens Jennifer Padgett and Natasha Bradley have set up shop showing the latest looks by Marc Jacobs, Jane Mayle, Tracey Feith, and Souchi, with shoes by Gunmetal and Richard Tyler and jewelry by Trish Becker. An editorial favorite, they are frequently spotted on the pages of Vogue, Elle, In Style and W, where their style has been described as "uptown girl meets rocker chick."

Suzanne, Natasha, Summer, Jennifer & Smokey

Mainline Gifts

Gift & Novelty Store

1928 Fillmore Street • San Francisco, CA 94115
415.563.4438 tel • 415.563.7528 fax
Fillmore

Open

Mon	10:00-7:00
Tues	10:00-7:00
Wed	10:00-7:00
Thurs	10:00-7:00
Fri	10:00-7:00
Sat	10:00-7:00
Sun	11:00-7:00

48

DENNIS URBIZTONDO

Established in 1968, the good-humored folks at Mainline Gifts have been bringing smiles to locals and visitors for over three decades. They carry a vast selection of gifts and novelties including everything from furniture and contemporary housewares, to games, jewelry, and bath products. They also stock greeting cards for everyone in your life: tasteful cards for Mom, and wicked-funny cards for friends and lovers. Shopping for gifts has never been so much fun.

Sue & Rich

Invision Optometry

Eye Glasses & Eye Care

1907 Fillmore Street • San Francisco, CA 94115
415.563.9003 tel • 415.563.9006 fax
www.citysearch.com/sfo/invisionopto
Fillmore

HELGA SIGVALDADOTTIR

Open

Mon	10:00-6:30
Tues	10:00-6:30
Wed	10:00-6:30
Thurs	10:00-6:30
Fri	10:00-6:30
Sat	10:00-6:30
Sun	12:00-4:00

49

Doctors Clifford and Edna Lee know that state-of-the-art eye care should be accompanied by extraordinary eyewear. At their Pacific Heights practice, they provide not only a full range of eye care services, but also stylish surroundings. More than 600 styles by frame designers Oliver Peoples, Paul Smith, Matsuda, Face A Face, and Kata are creatively displayed in the spacious location, which boasts high ceilings, skylights, a black-and-white checkered floor and exhibits of local artists' work gracing the walls. Invision takes pride in being known as a neighborhood business with a unique selection and top-notch customer service.

Dr. Clifford Lee, Dr. Edna Lee & Joseph Costa

Fillamento

Home Store

2185 Fillmore Street • San Francisco, CA 94115
415.931.2224 tel • 415.931.6304 fax
www.fillamento.com
Fillmore

Open

Mon	11:00-7:00
Tues	11:00-7:00
Wed	11:00-7:00
Thurs	11:00-7:00
Fri	11:00-7:00
Sat	11:00-7:00
Sun	12:00-6:00

50

FILLAMENTO COLLECTION

Iris Fuller

Fillamento has been a pioneer of bringing upscale home furnishings to the public since it first opened its doors in 1981. Now 20, San Francisco's premier home store continues to inspire its customers with a remarkable collection of design from all over the world. Owner and buyer Iris Fuller has been recognized for her amazing eye and impeccable taste, and the store enjoys a loyal following. Aptly named for its cross streets, Fillmore and Sacramento, Fillamento is filled with enticing displays that allow customers to experience and savor the store's selection and invites them to be creative in their own homes. The knowledgeable staff is yet another asset—bring them your most daunting decorating questions, and they'll help you find the perfect solutions. Visit Fillamento and fuel your imagination....

Hotel Majestic

Hotel

1500 Sutter Street • San Francisco, CA 94109
415.441.1100 tel • 415.673.7331 fax
www.thehotelmajestic.com
Fillmore/Cathedral Hill

HOTEL MAJESTIC COLLECTION

Brooks Bayly

51

The Hotel Majestic embodies the time-less glamour of the grand hotel. Built in 1902 and originally a private mansion, the Hotel was restored to its original opulence in the mid-'80s. The interiors boast English and French antiques, Biedermeier chairs, and alabaster and bronze chandeliers. This is a place where both visitors and locals can feel like royalty. Treat yourself to the warm hospitality and the graceful surroundings of a bygone age. Here, you can take a well-earned vacation, host and impress your business colleagues, or dine on exquisitely prepared California cuisine. While sipping your martini at the 19th century mahogany bar, scope out the rare butterfly collection, savor the Old World atmosphere, and re-create the wonder of your first San Francisco visit, how you knew then you'd never want to leave.

Kiku Imports

Antique Furniture

1420 Sutter Street • San Francisco, CA 94109
415.929.8278 tel • 415.929.0607 fax
www.kikuimports.com
Fillmore/Cathedral Hill

Open

Mon	10:00-6:00
Tues	10:00-6:00
Wed	10:00-6:00
Thurs	10:00-6:00
Fri	10:00-6:00
Sat	10:00-6:00
Sun	10:00-6:00

TEENA ALBERT

With reproductions of Asian designs flooding furniture outlets, Kiku Japanese Antiques is a treasure trove of authenticity. The spacious Japantown showroom specializes in tansu (broadly defined as furniture, specifically as traditional chests) but also carries late 18th century to early 20th century antiques, keepsakes, folk crafts (mingei), decorative items and textiles. Owner Akira Gomi opened Kiku 15 years ago, and still travels to Japan to procure merchandise. In fact, the staff never knows exactly what to expect from each shipment, and often receives objects that defy classification. A second-floor warehouse that carries "as is" tansu is also open to the public.

Shay Cameron, Manager

Costumes on Haight

Costume Shop

735 Haight Street • San Francisco, CA 94117
415.621.1356 tel • 415.621.4985 fax
www.citysearch.com/sfo/costumeshaight
Haight

Open
Mon   11:00-7:00
Tues   11:00-7:00
Wed   11:00-7:00
Thurs 11:00-7:00
Fri   11:00-7:00
Sat   11:00-7:00
Sun   12:00-6:0 0

53

Looking for a good disguise? For Halloween? A costume party? A masquerade ball? Dinner with the family? Costumes on Haight carries everything you need to standout or hide out. Superhero to sultry starlet, fairy godmother to gangster, you'll find an abundance of identities crammed under one roof along with quick-fix accessories like wigs and makeup. And with an average rental fee of $30, you can even indulge your multiple personalities—maybe a nun one week and Madonna the next. How about a Raggedy Ann/Godzilla combination? Just an idea.

**Aron, John,
Jerry & Danny**

Satellite

Vintage Clothing & Home Furnishings

1364 Haight Street • San Francisco, CA 94117
415.626.1364 tel
www.satellitevintage.com
Haight

Open

Mon	12:00-7:00
Tues	12:00-7:00
Wed	12:00-7:00
Thurs	12:00-7:00
Fri	12:00-7:00
Sat	11:00-7:00
Sun	12:00-6:30

54

JACKI TAYLOR

Step back in time and enter Satellite, a vintage clothing and furnishings store with a selection of new items from local artists. Owners Jacki Taylor and Jason Cowan started Satellite to provide a link to the past, and an opportunity for environmentally responsible shopping. The goods in their store cover most of the last century, from the '20s to the early '80s, from tees to tuxedos. Whatever you're looking for, you'll find it here— flapper fringe, rodeo chic or disco glam. Tucked among the chrome dinettes, lamps, and other home furnishings, are pulp fiction novels. Let the dramatic, campy covers provide the inspiration for your next knockout outfit.

Jacki Taylor & Jason Cowan

Behind the Post Office

Women's Apparel

1510 Haight Street • San Francisco, CA 94117
415.861.2507 tel • 415.861.2575 fax
www.behindthepostoffice.com
Haight

HELGA SIGVALDADÓTTIR

Open

Mon	11:00-7:00
Tues	11:00-7:00
Wed	11:00-7:00
Thurs	11:00-7:00
Fri	11:00-7:00
Sat	11:00-7:00
Sun	11:00-7:00

55

Kim Baskind

In the heart of the Haight District, you'll find Behind the Post Office. Shopping in this cozy boutique is like shopping in your coolest girlfriend's closet, discovering a vast collection of the latest, hippest designers. Owners Kim Baskind and Stephen Pringle are always on the lookout for young talent, which is why both locals and tourists flock to this destination store to catch the latest styles. They carry an impressive selection of sexy tees, and casual street clothes. Clothing lines include Development, Seven, Joes, Michael Stars, Ulla Johnson, and Lauren Moffatt. They also feature designer shoes by Goffredo Fantini, Florence Girardier, and others.

Happy Trails

Gift & Novelty Store

1615 Haight Street • San Francisco, CA 94117
415.431.7232 tel
www.niftygifty.com
Haight

Open

Mon	11:00-7:30
Tues	11:00-7:30
Wed	11:00-7:30
Thurs	11:00-7:30
Fri	11:00-7:30
Sat	11:00-7:30
Sun	11:00-7:30

Emeline & Mom, Gretchen

In the heart of the Haight is a bit of consummate Americana called Happy Trails. This "one-stop pop shop" merges Western flair with camp giddiness. Fuzzy dice dangle beside cowboy hats, dashboard hula dolls dance near rodeo attire. Happy Trails was founded by Gretchen McMann-Chapman, whose favorite cowboy is her dad. She began her business by scouring Midwest thrift stores and estate sales, eventually adding pop-culture items like Elvis wall clocks and fancy footwear like flamed creepers. The result is a fun, snappy mix of raucousness and rockabilly. At Happy Trails, jest meets West.

Taxi

Women's Apparel

1615 Haight Street • San Francisco, CA 94117
415.431.9614 tel
Haight

HELGA SIGVALDADÓTTIR

Open

Mon	11:00-7:30
Tues	11:00-7:30
Wed	11:00-7:30
Thurs	11:00-7:30
Fri	11:00-7:30
Sat	11:00-7:30
Sun	11:00-7:30

On a street known for its counter-cultural bent, Taxi offers a hip haven of sophisticated styles from up-and-coming and underground designers. The long, narrow space, sparsely decorated with color-washed wooden furniture and other feminine accents, is the perfect showcase for the sensuous, close-fitting pieces from the likes of Liz Collins and Eley Kishimoto. The boutique's clientele tends to be artists, stylists, actresses and others who place a high premium on the personality and individual looks of lines like Alice Roi's modern take on the '80s.

Debbie & daughter, Emeline

Sybil

Women's Apparel

1687 Haight Street • San Francisco, CA 94117
1858 Union Street •San Francisco, CA 94123
415.703.0498 tel (Haight) • 415.474.1981 tel (Cow Hollow/Marina)
Haight & Cow Hollow/Marina

Open

Mon	11:00-7:00
Tues	11:00-7:00
Wed	11:00-7:00
Thurs	11:00-7:00
Fri	11:00-7:00
Sat	11:00-7:00
Sun	11:00-7:00

58

HEATHER DE KONING

Sybil is a hip destination store for locals and trendsetter from New York and Los Angeles. A favorite with the film and music industry and stylists, Sybil has two locations, each with its own unique modern design. Each store carries different merchandise and both offer a mix of current sought after favorites like Earl Jean, Chaiken, and Paul and Joe—as well as young up and coming designers. These boutiques appeal to the trendy clientelle looking for the latest styles or the more unique edgy items. Appointments/personal shoppers are available.

Bullet Proof

Men's & Women's Apparel

629 Haight Street • San Francisco, CA 94117
415.255.7168 tel • 415.255.7168 fax
www.bulletproof.com
Haight

HELGA SIGVALDADOTTIR

Open

Tues	12:00-7:00
Wed	12:00-7:00
Thurs	12:00-7:00
Fri	12:00-7:00
Sat	12:00-7:00
Sun	12:00-7:00

Maria Eder

Known to locals as the place to pick up the latest fashion and tickets to the famous "Boat Party" (a party on a boat sailing the Bay with live bands—phone the store for more details), Bullet Proof is celebrating its 10th anniversary. Though the fashion at Bullet Proof is always cutting edge—if not a bit ahead of its time—the shop retains the free-spirited attitude of the Haight, circa 1968. Here, you'll find men's and women's clothing by local and international designers. Everything from funky street clothes to elegant formalwear, and at good prices too. They also stock a great selection of tee shirts, including the iconic Bullet Proof logo tee.

Zeitgeist Timepieces

Watches & Watch Repair

437 B Hayes Street • San Francisco, CA 94102
415.864.0185 tel
Hayes Valley

Open

Tues	12:00-6:00
Wed	12:00-6:00
Thurs	12:00-6:00
Fri	12:00-6:00
Sat	12:00-6:00

HELGA SIGVALDADÓTTIR

The first watch was invented in 1524. So it is a time-honored, centuries-old tradition which Marc Garman and Carsten Marsch draw on at Zeitgeist Timepieces and Jewelry. Master watchmakers and jewelers with a combined 40 years in the trade, they can refurbish your Rolex or reset your rubies. Or, if you're going for a new look altogether, choose from the vast collection of vintage wrist and pocket watches dating back to the 1920s. You can also get a glimpse of Marc and Carsten in their workshop, bringing old family treasures and newer timepieces back to life.

Marc & Carsten

The Painters Place

Custom Framing

371 Hayes Street • San Francisco, CA 94102
415.431.9827 tel • 415.431.7113 fax
www.thepaintersplace.com
Hayes Valley

TOM PAINTER

Open

Mon	10:00-4:00
Tues	10:00-6:00
Wed	10:00-6:00
Thurs	10:00-6:00
Fri	10:00-6:00
Sat	10:00-4:00

61

It begins with your basic rectangle, that ubiquitous shape that defines borders, supports content, and represents both format and challenge to any frame shop. At the Painters Place in Hayes Valley, the rectangle is reinvented daily. With over 5,000 frame samples available and several woodworkers and gilders on staff, The Painters Place has the raw materials and in-house talent to design the crowning complement for any two- (or three-) dimensional object you may wish to display and admire. (They also build stands and bases.) Their standards of excellence are uncompromising, and that's one reason why their customers include SFMOMA, art galleries, corporate collectors, and private collectors. Fulfilling the prophecy of his name, landscape artist Stan Painter started the shop with his wife Pat in 1963; son Matt bought the business in 1995 and now runs it with brother Tom. They still sell their father's paintings and have obviously inherited his creative skill. At the Painters Place, a rectangle— or any other shape—is a source of inspiration.

Dan, Amrit & Gary

Champp de Mars

Antiques & Home Furnishing

347 Hayes Street • San Francisco, CA 94102
415.252.9434 tel • 415.252.9434 fax
Hayes Valley

Open

Tues	11:00-6:30
Wed	11:00-6:30
Thurs	11:00-6:30
Fri	11:00-6:30
Sat	11:00-6:30
Sun	12:00-5:00

62

HELGA SIGVALDADÓTTIR

Pierre, Marceau & Louis

Francophiles are in for a treat at Champ de Mars. A few years back, Lyon natives Pierre Moskovtchenko and Marceau Galliot packed up their antique business and moved to Hayes Valley, where they've re-created the warm, welcoming spirit found in a French country home. With toys, country antiques, dishes, linens and items such as jam pots and dog portraits packed within its bold red and gray walls, Champ de Mars also feels like a French flea market. Antiques from the 18th and 19th centuries, the height of French decorative arts, are a particular specialty at this business that embodies the French art of living.

wOrldware

Home Furnishings

336 Hayes Street • San Francisco, CA 94102
415.487.9030 tel • 415.487.9032 fax
www.worldwaresf.com
Hayes Valley

Open

Mon	11:00-6:00
Tues	11:00-6:00
Wed	11:00-6:00
Thurs	11:00-6:00
Fri	11:00-6:00
Sat	11:00-6:00
Sun	12:00-5:00

CRUCITA POLIZZI

63

Interior designer Greg Henson and Jeff Brooks have created Worldware, a sophisticated, luxurious collection of home furnishings, gifts, and accessories collected from around the world. Custom crafted mohair sofas, French leather club chairs, Italian rugs, silk bedding from Morocco and hundreds of accessories are just the beginning of your journey through Worldware. In addition, some of the best bath products and gift items are available. French milled soaps, Italian moulding picture frames, hand made tassels, and plush towels from Switzerland, to name a few. Worldware also provides interior design services to its customers, from their cutting edge design team.

**Greg & Jeff,
Rison & Carmel**

Alla Prima

Lingerie

539 Hayes Street • San Francisco, CA 94102
1420 Grant Avenue • San Francisco, CA 94133
415.864.8180 tel (Hayes Valley) • 415.397.4077 tel (North Beach)
www.allaprima.net
Hayes Valley & North Beach

Open:

Mon	11:00-7:00
Tues	11:00-7:00
Wed	11:00-7:00
Thurs	11:00-7:00
Fri	11:00-7:00
Sat	11:00-7:00
Sun	12:00-5:00

Yolaida Duran & Lily Hsia

Alla Prima presents fine lingerie in a setting that is warm and inviting. Two locations, in Hayes Valley and North Beach, engage the senses and celebrate the body. The lingerie has been carefully selected to meet the needs and sensibilities of modern women. At Alla Prima, women are encouraged to explore a personal language of style and attitude through lingerie. Co-owners Yolaida and Lily are always on hand to guide clientele toward the correct fit and form. Both stores specialize in lingerie from Europe (La Perla, Aubade, Lise Charmel, Gemma, Hanro, Wolford, Eres, et al), but also feature sleepwear, jewelry, and a line of hand-blended perfumes. Emerging designers are also showcased. The Hayes Valley location offers one of the best selections of swimwear in the City. After a visit to Alla Prima's opulent dressing room with its torchére lamps and overstuffed settee, you may just find yourself feeling more elegant, sexier, or simply transformed.

Manifesto:

Men's & Women's Apparel
514 Octavia Street • San Francisco, CA 94102
415.431.4778 tel • 415.437.0699 fax
retro514@wt.net
Hayes Valley

TOM ONTIVEROS

Open

Wed	10:00-6:00
Thurs	10:00-7:00
Fri	10:00-6:00
Sat	11:00-6:00
Sun	12:00-5:00

65

Designers Sarah Franko and Suzanne Castillo have revamped vintage clothing to define their own contemporary versions of those classic, comfortable garments of the '40s and '50s. They make and sell their creations at Manifesto:, their studio/boutique in Hayes Valley. It's all here: two tones, floral prints, muted plaids, full-cut trousers. These are the kind of clothes Sinatra donned when kicking back between gigs, the sort of country-meets-city fashion Monroe flaunted by the poolside. Its a gangster-glamour, casino-casual aesthetic that has a timelessness all its own. If there's a rallying cry for Manifesto:, it would be this: Viva Las Vegas!

Suzanne & Sarah

Coulars

Women's Apparel

327 Hayes Street • San Francisco, CA 94102
415.255.2925 tel • 415.255.2980 fax
www.citysearch.com/sfo/coularsboutique
Hayes Valley

Open
Mon	11:00-6:00
Tues	11:00-6:00
Wed	11:00-6:00
Thurs	11:00-6:00
Fri	11:00-6:00
Sat	12:00-6:00

66

HELGA SIGVALDADOTTIR

Marijke Coulars

Where can you find fabulously designed clothes and helpful advice? At Coulars in Hayes Valley. A contemporary designer boutique for women, this shop is filled with wearable knits, versatile fabrics, and unique details—a flirty color, a flared sleeve, a flashy button. Designers include Ines Raspoort, Le Nar NV, Margie Tsai, Patina, Amy Rigg, Krista Larson, Dinn, Monika Turtle, and 3 Dots. They also carry jewelry by Simone Coulars and Nicolette Gamache. The shop's Dutch-born owner, Marijke Coulars, applies her taste and talent not only to selecting her merchandise but to helping her customers choose the right styles and fit. With her infectious enthusiasm and energy, Coulars provides an unbeatable combination—friendly fashion and a fashion friend. Marijke will always make you look good.

Dark Garden

Corsets & Wedding Gowns

321 Linden Street • San Francisco, CA 94102
415.431.7684 tel
www.darkgarden.com
Hayes Valley

PETER DA SILVA

Open

Mon	10:00-6:00
Tues	10:00-6:00
Wed	10:00-6:00
Thurs	10:00-6:00
Fri	10:00-6:00
Sat	11:00-5:00
Sun	12:00-4:00

Autumn

Dark Garden proprietress Autumn Carey-Adamme has been sewing her entire life. After making her first corset at age 12, she says she was hooked. By 16 she was studying costume design and apprenticing with a couturier; by 18 she opened her own shop. The mission of Dark Garden is to offer a comfortable, non-judgmental environment where imaginative visions can take shape. Most designs are made to order. The customer selects the style and fabric, then 12 measurements are taken to give each garment that second-skin fit. Clientele include conservatives with a fantasy, drag queens, professional dominants and their submissives, and anyone curious.

Alabaster

Home Furnishings

597 Hayes Street • San Francisco, CA 94102
415.558.0482 tel • 415.558.0587 fax
www.alabastersf.com
Hayes Valley

Open

Tues	11:00-6:00
Wed	11:00-6:00
Thurs	11:00-6:00
Fri	11:00-6:00
Sat	11:00-6:00
Sun	12:00-5:00

68

HELGA SIGVALDADOTTIR

Nelson Bloncourt

Alabaster, an airy, bright home furnishings store in Hayes Valley, is an eclectic mixture of antiques, fine arts, and contemporary items. Owners Nelson Bloncourt and Paul Davis are guided in their selections by a sense of timeless style and a taste for the offbeat. Their eye-pleasing displays include alabaster lamps, mother-of-pearl flatware, French ivory boxes, Venetian mirrors, sleek aluminum furniture, and hand-tinted photographs. Like the near-white mineral it's named for, Alabaster is awash in creams and whites with strokes of occasional color throughout—vintage globes in descending size order, an arrangement of batiked eggs, or a pile of small-art-press books. The overall effect is a harmonious mingling of styles, periods, and materials. At Alabaster, let your eyes lead you—you can't go astray.

Deborah Hampton

Women's Apparel

555 Hayes Street • San Francisco, CA 94102
415.701.8682 tel • 415.701.9072 fax
Hayes Valley

Open	
Tues	11:00-7:00
Wed	11:00-7:00
Thurs	11:00-7:00
Fri	11:00-7:00
Sat	11:00-7:00
Sun	12:00-6:00

PAUL MOORE

Anyone who lives in or visits San Francisco recognizes the inherent chic of the place. But it took the arrival of Deborah Hampton (via England and New York) to transform the city from stylish metropolis to international fashion center. Her design sensibility was shaped by stints with Calvin Klein and Michael Kors, consummate American artists both. Like her mentors, Hampton's is not strictly runway fashion; it's a combination of luxurious fabrics, simple lines, and exquisite tailoring suited to anyone who wants to make an understated but lasting impression. Her designs will quickly become your favorite staple items: garments that look good and feel good, the mark of classic American design. Deborah Hampton crossed an ocean and a continent to get here, but it seems she has found her home.

Deborah Hampton

Zeni

Men's & Women's Apparel

567 Hayes Street • San Francisco, CA 94102
415.864.0154 tel • 415.558.0467 fax
Hayes Valley

Open

Mon	12:00-7:00
Tues	12:00-7:00
Wed	12:00-7:00
Thurs	12:00-7:00
Fri	12:00-7:00
Sat	11:00-7:00
Sun	11:00-6:00

HELGA SIGVALDADÓTTIR

Leshawn

Time to ditch all your dull duds and adopt a little attitude. You'll find everything you need at Zeni in Hayes Valley. With a reputation for catching trends before they crest, Zeni carries men's and women's clothing that declares its message loud and clear: "fashion first!" This designer boutique owned by Daniel Bacon targets the contemporary, cutting-edge customer and doesn't miss. Labels include BCBG, FTX, Armand Basi, Tessuto, Nicole Miller, Anna Sui, and Zeni's own women's line. Of course, no attitude would be complete without sunglasses. Choose from shades from Dita, Stussy, Smith, and others. Now that you have the attire and accessories, go out and intimidate some people.

Pomp Home

Home Furnishings

516 Hayes Street • San Francisco, CA 94102
415.864.1830 tel • 415.864.1830 fax
Hayes Valley

HELGA SIGVALDADOTTIR

Open

Mon	12:00-7:00
Tues	12:00-7:00
Wed	12:00-7:00
Thurs	12:00-7:00
Fri	12:00-7:00
Sat	12:00-7:00
Sun	12:00-5:00

Contemporary, can mean many things, but at Pomp Home, it means furnishings and accessories that appeal to an urban, design-conscious, trendy sensibility. Günter Frivert, a native of Vienna, started Pomp Home 8 years ago in trendy Hayes Valley. Carrying a surprisingly affordable selection of everything from couches, chairs, and dishware to posters, vases, books and candles, the hip store is a veritable lifestyle boutique. So relax into the leather furniture, pick up that nearby art book and consider the transformative potential of a Jonathan Adler pillow or Umbra frame.

Günter Frivert

Polanco

Arts & Crafts Gallery

393 Hayes Street • San Francisco, CA 94102
415.252.5753 tel • 415.252.5665 fax
Hayes Valley

Open

Mon	11:00-6:00
Tues	11:00-6:00
Wed	11:00-6:00
Thurs	11:00-6:00
Fri	11:00-6:00
Sat	11:00-6:00
Sun	1:00-6:00

72

ALDO PICCHI

Named for a district in Mexico City, Polanco is a gallery/shrine devoted to the fine and folk arts of our southern neighbors. This is the only Bay Area gallery representing Mexican artists exclusively and exhibitions cover work by contemporary luminaries such as Nahum Zenil and Rudolfo Morales as well as pieces from emerging artists. The folk art selection boasts traditional items made especially for Polanco from the Families Linares, de la Cruz, and Aguilar. Of course, there are also the unusual antiques—retablos, sculpture, and jewelry. Polanco was started by partners Aldo Picchi and John Camarillo, who fell in love with Mexico's rich artistic traditions during their south-of-the-border travels. Now San Francisco shoppers can benefit from their discoveries and Hayes Valley is a bit more colorful for their efforts.

Aldo Picchi & John Camarilo

Buu

Home Furnishings & Women's Apparel

506 Hayes Street • San Francisco, CA 94102
415.626.1503 tel • 415.626.1532 fax
buusf@yahoo.com
Hayes Valley

HELGA SIGVALDADÓTTIR

Open

Mon	12:00-7:00
Tues	12:00-7:00
Wed	12:00-7:00
Thurs	11:00-7:00
Fri	11:00-7:00
Sat	11:00-7:00
Sun	12:00-6:00

73

A passion for superlative design guides Buu. Inspired by her travels and guided by experience in industrial and interior design, owner Roxy Buu started this lifestyle boutique 4 years ago as a way to seek out and sell great designs. To that end, her compact store carries Japanese, European, and American objects, including dishes, glassware, gifts, watches, candles, soaps and incense, and select fashion-forward women's apparel. Amid the well-balanced store's collection of sculptural objects and unique offerings, shoppers may also encounter Mongy, Buu's resident Pug. Can a spread in Wallpaper be far off?

Mongy

Bucheon Gallery

Art Gallery

540 Hayes Street • San Francisco, CA 94102
415.863.2891 tel • 415.861.0478 fax
www.bucheon.com
Hayes Valley

Open
Wed 11:00-6:00
Thurs 11:00-6:00
Fri   11:00-6:00
Sat   11:00-6:00
Sun 12:00-5:00

74

DAN EASTON

I f you want in on the pulse of the San Francisco art scene, walk through the doors of Bucheon Gallery. Staging 10 exhibits a year, the gallery specializes in nurturing the talents of the Bay Area's brightest emerging and mid-career artists. Despite the fine art focus, the Gallery manages to keep a homey feel, thanks in part to co-directors Sheila Cohen and Sidney Brown's frisky pups, which greet visitors at the door. Sheila credits the gallery's success to its central Hayes Valley location. Being surrounded by the ballet, opera, symphony, and inner-city neighborhoods brings a diverse variety of people to the gallery to view and discuss art. And with very reasonable prices and payment plans available, Bucheon Gallery may be the place to take home the next Diebenkorn or Thiebaud.

Ari & Ben

Velvet da Vinci

Art Gallery

508 Hayes Street • San Francisco, CA 94102
415.626.7478 tel • 415.386.2492 fax
www.velvetdavinci.com
Hayes Valley

HELGA SIGVALDADÓTTIR

Open

Tues	12:00-6:00
Wed	12:00-6:00
Thurs	12:00-6:00
Fri	12:00-6:00
Sat	12:00-6:00
Sun	12:00-4:00

75

A cornerstone of the revitalized Hayes Valley shopping district, Velvet da Vinci Gallery exclusively presents art jewelry and sculpture like you have never seen anywhere else. Owners Mike Holmes and Elizabeth Shypertt select beautiful one-of-a-kind artwork, as well as fine production pieces, handmade by skilled and creative jewelers and metalsmiths from San Francisco as well as Europe and Japan. You will find everything from rings, brooches, and necklaces to tiaras, kinetic sculpture, and life-size wire people. Frequent special exhibitions ensure that you will see interesting new work every time you visit. The quality and range of work shown at Velvet da Vinci has made it a regular must-see stop for collectors, museum curators, and other knowledge-able art and art-jewelry enthusiasts.

**Mike Holmes &
Elizabeth Shypertt**

Citizen Cake

Restaurant/Patisserie

399 Grove Street • San Francisco, CA 94102
415.861.2228 tel • 415.861.0565 fax
www.citizencake.com
Hayes Valley

Open

Tues	7:00-10:00
Wed	7:00-10:00
Thurs	7:00-10:00
Fri	7:00-10:00
Sat	9:00-10:00
Sun	9:00-10:00

MAREN CARUSO

Elizabeth Falkner

Eat something extraordinary—everyday. This is the mission of Citizen Cake, a restaurant/patisserie in Hayes Valley. Citizen Cake is the creation of pastry chef Elizabeth Falkner (who learned her craft at Masa's, Elka, and Rubicon). Here, you can imbibe various caffeine concoctions, linger over afternoon tea, American-style, or meander through dinner—whether you are off to the Opera or not. But be sure to leave room for the main act: dessert. Falkner, schooled in film at the San Francisco Art Institute, brings cinematic inspiration, surprising ingredients, and architectural flair to her constructions. Cakes include A Chocolate Work Orange, Retro Tropical Shag, and After Midnight. And, of course, Falkner, the culinary genius pays tribute to Welles, the cinematic genius, with Citizen Cake's signature "Rosebud"—a rose-scented crème brulee tart.

Japonesque

Art Gallery

824 Montgomery Street • San Francisco, CA 94133
415.391.8860 tel • 415.391.3530 fax
Jackson Square

ALAN WEISSKOPF

Open

Tues	10:30-5:30
Wed	10:30-5:30
Thurs	10:30-5:30
Fri	10:30-5:30
Sat	11:00-5:00

77

To enter Koichi Hara's spacious, Jackson Square gallery is to enter another world. Although Japonesque carries many everyday items such as furniture and tableware along with antiques and art, everything is displayed so exquisitely that the two-level gallery feels like a sanctuary. Each object has breathing space—ma—whether it's a stone sculpture by Masatoshi Izumi or a black lacquered bowl. Hara believes that beauty can be found in useful objects inspired by nature. Clay, wood, bamboo, iron, bronze, and linen are also common materials in the gallery's objects, some of which are commissioned from Japanese craftsmen and artists. Visiting the gallery may inspire you to rethink the relationship between living and aesthetics. And that's just the sort of epiphany Hara hopes Japonesque will inspire.

Koichi Hara

William Stout Architectural Books

Book Store

804 Montgomery Street • San Francisco, CA 94133
27-A South Park • San Francisco, CA 94107
415.391.6757 tel (Jackson Square) • 415.495.6757 tel (SOMA)
www.stoutbooks.com
Jackson Square & SOMA

Open: Jackson Square

Mon	10:00-6:30
Tues	10:00-6:30
Wed	10:00-6:30
Thurs	10:00-6:30
Fri	10:00-6:30
Sat	10:00-5:30

Open: SOMA

Tues	11:00-5:30
Wed	11:00-5:30
Thurs	11:00-5:30
Fri	11:00-5:30
Sat	11:30-5:00

CESAR RUBIO

Bill Stout

Williiam Stout Architectural Books has built its international reputation and a good deal of its interior construction on that most irresistible of commodities—books. (This despite the Web wave.) Front to back, floor to ceiling. The shelves are an architectural wonder unto themselves. Bill Stout started his business back in the '70s, selling books out of his living room. Eventually he needed a separate site, opened in Jackson Square in 1974. (The South Park location was added in 1999.) In addition to every type of architectural volume, William Stout also stocks books on urban planning, landscaping, interior and industrial design, furniture, graphics, art, and photography.

Ruby Gallery

Gift Store

3602 20th Street • San Francisco, CA 94110
415.550.8052 tel
www.rubygallery.com
Mission

LAURA JAMES

Open

Tues	3:00-7:00
Wed	12:00-7:00
Thurs	12:00-7:00
Fri	12:00-7:00
Sat	11:00-6:00
Sun	11:00-6:00

79

Laura & Ruby

Voted best place to buy gifts and jewelry by the San Francisco Bay Guardian, Ruby Gallery is a melange of eclectic crafts and artful treasures, all from Bay Area artists. Owner Laura James has a vision of artists being able to support themselves making art as well as a conviction that people need beautiful objects to thrive. Behold Ruby Gallery. Here, there's something for every budget and sensibility. You'll find fine jewelry and art glass, paintings and pillows, beaded lamps, even handmade cards. Ruby Gallery loves local artists, and you will too.

Laku

Gift Store

1069 Valencia Street • San Francisco, CA 94110
415.695.1462 tel • 415.695.1462 fax
lakuyaeko@aol.com
Mission

Open
Tues 11:30-6:30
Wed 11:30-6:30
Thurs 11:30-6:30
Fri   11:30-6:30
Sat   11:3 0-6:30
Sun   12:00-5:00

80

SHUNKA TOYAMA

Yaeko

Laku, located along the revitalized Valencia corridor, is a treasure chest of fabric wonders—flowing silk scarves, cunning wool cloches, body-skimming knit tops. The artist behind these wearable confections is Yaeko Yamashita, who can turn every fiber or bauble into an object of beauty. She named the shop for her son, and there is an air of loving care about the place. You'll be loath to leave without treating yourself to one of Yaeko's creations, perhaps a pair of the elfin velvet slippers, which she can make to order. These are tempting enough in grown-up sizes, but utterly irresistible in the child versions you can hold in your palm. The next baby in your life needs these.

Rayon Vert

Floral Design & Home Furnishings

3187 16th Street • San Francisco, CA 94103
415.861.3516 tel • 415.861.2468 fax
Mission

CESAR RUBIO

Open
Wed 12:00-6:00
Thurs 12:00-6:00
Fri 12:00-6:00
Sat 12:00-6:00

Kelly

In the midst of the urban Mission District, Rayon Vert offers a place to stop and smell the roses—among other beautiful blooms. Six years ago, owner Kelly Kornegay opened a floral design studio that has evolved into a gift and retail store as well. Here, oversized letters in the front window spelling out "Open" or "Nope" mark the hours; inside, the spacious environment feels like a garden with beautiful arrangements of flowers merchandised amongst the stores' wares. You'll find bath products, apothecary jars, French vases, beeswax and scented candles, industrial furniture, cards, books, and artwork by local artists. With the motto "extraordinary flowers, extraordinary home," Rayon Vert is the perfect spot to shop for distinctive gifts and artful, garden-style floral arrangements. A Floral delivery service is available Monday through Saturday.

Good Vibrations

Erotic Shop

1210 Valencia Street • San Francisco, CA 94110
415.974.8980 tel • 415.550.8495 fax
www.goodvibes.com
Mission

Open

Mon	11:00-7:00
Tues	11:00-7:00
Wed	11:00-8:00
Thurs	11:00-8:00
Fri	11:00-8:00
Sat	11:00-8:00
Sun	11:00-8:00

82

ELISA GALDO, MARTHA JONES

If ever there were a feel good business, Good Vibrations would be it. Let us count the ways. Dedicated to sexual health and pleasure, Good Vibrations stocks sex toys, books, audiotapes, and videos designed to stimulate the body *and* the imagination. The store, founded in 1988 and worker-owned since 1992, is known for its friendly and knowledgeable staff. They take quality control seriously, and most everything in Good Vibrations is personally tested, viewed, and read for safety, accuracy, and effectiveness. They even sponsor outreach presentations in the community to dispel myths and promote safe sex. It's an open, honest, easygoing environment you'll encounter at Good Vibrations, one in which you can feel comfortable and ask questions. You'll feel good as soon as you enter their Valencia Street location or Berkeley store and even better once you get home with your wares.

Eyedare Optometric

Eye Glasses & Eye Care

3122 16th Street • San Francisco, CA 94103
415.241.0240 tel • 415.241.0523 fax
www.eyedare.com
Mission

JENNIFER KEY

Open

Mon	11:00-7:00
Tues	11:00-7:00
Wed	11:00-7:00
Thurs	11:00-7:00
Fri	9:00-5:00
Sat	9:00-5:00

83

In true San Francisco style, Eyedare puts the focus on fashion. The whimsical window displays at this optometry shop wouldn't look out of place at a hip art gallery. Inside, leather cube furniture and an ultra-cool magazine selection invites customers to relax in the sun-drenched corner shop at 16th and Guerrero streets. Together, San Francisco native Dr. Chester Quan and his fellow doctors offer more than 20 years of comprehensive eye care experience. They carry designer eyewear from Europe and Japan, including frames by LA Eyeworks, Lafont, Hiero, Calvin Klein, Dita, and Alain Milkli, as well as an Eyedare line.

Ali & Dr. Quan

Encantada Gallery

Art Gallery & Gift Shop

904-908 Valencia Street • San Francisco, CA 94110
415.642.3939 tel • 415.642.3933 fax
encantadagallery@yahoo.com
Mission

Open

Tues	12:00-6:00
Wed	12:00-6:00
Thurs	12:00-6:00
Fri	12:00-8:00
Sat	12:00-8:00
Sun	12:00-6:00

84

ENCANTADA COLLECTION

Mia

Along lively Valencia Street, you'll find Encantada Fine Art Gallery. Encantada opened its doors in November 1997 with its first Dia de los Muertos exhibit, commemorating the Mexican celebration of death and renewal. This annual show is a mainstay of Encantada's events calendar that includes a variety of other exhibitions, workshops, and lectures. The companion gift shop, Arte Popular, offer the best in Mexican folk art—silver jewelry, Talavera pottery, textiles, religious icons, papeles picados, woodcarvings, and more items for home, office, and garden. Encantada Gallery takes its name from a Spanish greeting—literally "enchanted"—which pretty much sums up how you'll feel on a visit to this gallery.

Paxton Gate

Garden & Natural Science Store

824 Valencia Street • San Francisco, CA 94110
415.824.1872 tel • 415.824.1871 fax
www.paxton-gate.com
Mission

JENNY DOLL

85

Sean Quigley

Open	
Mon	12:00-7:00
Tues	12:00-7:00
Wed	12:00-7:00
Thurs	12:00-7:00
Fri	12:00-7:00
Sat	12:00-7:00
Sun	12:00-7:00

Part natural history museum, part art gallery, part gardener's paradise, Paxton Gate offers a variety of oddities, useful tools, and outdoorsy services linked by one overriding theme: nature. Sean Quigley, the brains and heart behind the operation, has taken his fascination with the natural world in every possible direction. Paxton Gate's goods include such seemingly divergent items as mounted insects, Japanese pruning shears, stuffed rattlesnakes and toads, Ikebana accessories, fossils, and gardening books. Peruse the selection of unusual orchids and epiphytes to add a touch of the exotic to you garden or home. Or if plants wither in you presence, leave it to the experts and enlist Quigley's landscaping services. Paxton Gate also hosts lectures on entomology, flower arranging, taxidermy, and edible insects. Let's see what a nature boy or girl you can be.

Home Remedies

Home Furnishings

1026 Valencia Street • San Francisco, CA 94110
415.826.2026 tel • 415.826.2080 fax
www.bradcochair.com
Mission

Open

Tues	12:00-7:00
Wed	12:00-7:00
Thurs	12:00-7:00
Fri	12:00-7:00
Sat	11:00-6:00
Sun	12:00-5:00

HELGA SIGVALDADÓTTIR

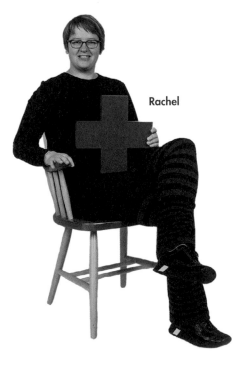

Rachel

New England has moved into the Mission in the form of Home Remedies, a store that specializes in classic American home furnishings. Owner Rachel Ambrose draws on her family's Maine woodworking company to provide simple, durable furniture made of solid hardwords like cherry, maple, and ash. Also featured is Maine Cottage Furniture, whose case pieces and upholstery are available in 40 fabulous colors. Bedding, bath products, lamps, art and cozy accessories round out this homey haven offering comfort to weary city dwellers. Re-design services are also available to help customers rework existing rooms and suggest new possibilities. As it is, you just might want to move in.

Scarlet Sage Herb Co.

Herb & Body Store

1173 Valencia Street • San Francisco, CA 94110
415.821.0997 tel • 415.821.0916 fax
www.scarletsageherb.com
Mission

HELGA SIGVALDADÓTTIR

Open	
Mon	11:00-6:30
Tues	11:00-6:30
Wed	11:00-6:30
Thurs	11:00-6:30
Fri	11:00-6:30
Sat	11:00-6:00
Sun	12:00-6:00

As soon as your enter the Scarlet Sage Herb Co., an herbal apothecary, you'll be soothed and transported as you take in the healing powers of more than 300 herbs, essential oils, and essences. Co-owners and herbalists Dino Lucas and Lisa Kellman research and stock the highest quality organic herbs and natural body care products available. Scarlet Sage also carries a wonderful selection of handmade, plant-inspired gifts such as aromatherapy candles, bath oils, and books on herbs and plants. Their commitment to healing extends beyond the merchandise to include personalized attention, regular classes, and tarot readings. Whether you're looking for a healing potion or a special gift, Scarlet Sage Herb Company has your remedy.

Dino & Lisa

Fishbowl

Men's & Women's Apparel

3253 Valencia Street • San Francisco, CA 94110
415.934.1726 tel • 415.934.1726 fax
fishbowl16@earthlink.net
Mission

Open

Tues	12:00-6:00
Wed	12:00-6:00
Thurs	12:00-6:00
Fri	12:00-7:00
Sat	12:00-7:00

Adrian & Milo

ADRIAN LEONG

Hipsters who troll the city in search of a fashion fix are always satisfied after a visit to Fishbowl. Just a stonesthrow from the epicenter of the Mission, at Fishbowl, you'll find an eclectic array of clothing by established and emerging designers. Combining bold colors and stainless steel, designing couple Adrian and Colleen Leong's tiny store specializes in must have urban basics like cool T-shirts and cargo pants. This is an ideal spot for collecting casual street clothes—everything from simple understated pieces, to edgy items. Fishbowl encourages men and women to mix it up a little, and to have fun with fashion.

HRM Boutique

Men's & Women's Apparel

924 Valencia Street • San Francisco, CA 94110
415.642.0841 tel
Mission

HELGA SIGVALDADÓTTIR

89

Open

Tues	12:00-7:00
Wed	12:00-7:00
Thurs	12:00-7:00
Fri	12:00-8:00
Sat	12:00-8:00
Sun	12:00-6:00

Susan Hengst

A new arrival to the Mission District, HRM Boutique relates seamlessly to its environment. Owners Susan Hengst and Bob Scales met during a stint with Lat Naylor at *Think Tank,* where they fine-tuned their own design sensibilities. Though their designs are contemporary and occasionally edgy, their approach to fashion has a populist bent, with an emphasis on comfortable, well-crafted quality clothes that are made to last. Most of the work is done on the premises in the adjoining studio/workshop, and new pieces are put out every couple of weeks. Hengst and Scales draw from a variety of influences, everything from patterns from the '40s and '50s, to current fashion developments. But they never stray from their philosophy of "making clothes that don't over-shadow people."

Retrofit Vintage

Vintage Clothing

910 Valencia Street • San Francisco, CA 94110
415.550.1530 tel
retrofit@earthlink.net
Mission

Open

Mon	12:00-7:00
Tues	1:30-7:00
Wed	12:00-7:00
Thurs	1:30-8:00
Fri	12:00-8:00
Sat	12:00-8:00
Sun	12:00-7:00

ALISON HOEKSTRA

What distinguishes Retrofit Vintage from its recycled-clothing counterparts are its particular specialties and kitschy window displays. Specifically, you'll discover within its jam-packed walls the best selection of vintage coats in town—leopard prints, vinyl, leather—and a veritable library of Playboy magazines from the '60s and '70s. What coffee table couldn't use a little camp? Owners Audrey Wackerly and Alison Hoekstra assemble funky fashion displays from their eclectic merchandise, any of which could pass for a bygone era. (Think Quadrophenia.) At Retrofit Vintage, it's easy to add a bit of San Francisco's fashion history to your own turn-of-the century wardrobe.

Alison & Audrey

Dema

Women's Apparel

1038 Valencia Street • San Francisco, CA 94110
415.206.0500 tel • 415.206.0995 fax
godemago@yahoo.com
Mission

DEMA COLLECTION

Open

Mon	11:00-7:00
Tues	11:00-7:00
Wed	11:00-7:00
Thurs	11:00-7:00
Fri	11:00-7:00
Sat	11:00-7:00
Sun	12:00-6:00

Dema

After successful stints in Seattle and New York, fashion designer Dema decided to settle in San Francisco, where her clean lines and mod designs have found a loyal following. Perhaps it's the '60s connection that has resulted in such a good fit. The decade is an ongoing source of inspiration for Dema's updated designs, which incorporate bright colors and prints, versatile fabrics, and basic silhouettes. But what makes her garments so wearable is the distinctive combination of femininity and functionality—you can look like a girl without being forced to act like one. Dema's separates and dresses are available at her Valencia Street boutique, where you can often find her working on her next line. If you'd like something in another size or color, no problem. Dema can stitch it up for you.

Foreign Cinema

Restaurant

2534 Mission Street • San Francisco, CA 94110
415.648.7600 tel • 415.648.7669 fax
www.foreigncinema.com
Mission

Open

Tues	6:00-11:00
Wed	6:00-11:00
Thurs	6:00-11:00
Fri	6:00-11:00
Sat	6:00-11:00
Sun	6:00-11:00

FOREIGN CINEMA COLLECTION

Michael Hecht

There's a hidden city waiting to be discovered behind the facades and canopies of San Francisco. That's where you'll find Foreign Cinema, a celebration of food and film tucked in the middle of a Mission District block. Partners Jon Varnedoe (of Café du Nord and Bruno's) and Michael Hecht recognized the potential of this "lost space" and opened a contemporary French bistro which screens foreign classics, independent features, and animated shorts on its back wall. Chef Laurent Katgely serves up a delectable dinner menu of California/French fare while his black-board menu provides additional eating options. You can choose between al fresco dining in the courtyard or comfortable indoor seating on the ground floor or mezzanine (a "balcony" view). And with two bars, libations—classic cocktails and Foreign Cinema's own creations as well as an impressive wine list by Bruno Baglin—are always nearby. Discover the nightlife behind the nightlife—make a reservation at Foreign Cinema.

220₂ Oxygen Bar

Oxygen Bar

795 Valencia Street • San Francisco, CA 94110
415.255.2102 tel
www.2202bar.com
Mission

Open	
Tues	4:00-2:00
Wed	4:00-2:00
Thurs	4:00-2:00
Fri	4:00-2:00
Sat	4:00-2:00
Sun	12:00-8:00

HELGA SIGVALDADÓTTIR

Welcome to the Mission's coolest, bluest, funkiest lounge around. Not your typical bar, instead of serving tequila shots or whiskey sours, they serve cool oxygen, sweet aromatherapy, and all the herbal drinks you need to refresh your body and revitalize your mind. Sink back and float away while soothing beats provide the perfect companion for the ultimate in relaxation. Featuring a constantly changing gallery of local artists, this is the perfect spot to relax either before or after shopping, strolling or clubbing. There are no worries inside this blazing blue interior of rainbow lights, deep seats, and swirling scents. Come by at night to tune into top-notch DJ talent scratching the turns off the tables, and a rump-bumping crowd. The staff is friendly and knowledgeable and will make certain you have a "purely intoxicating" experience.

Visa, Kim & Garth

Getups

New & Vintage Apparel

4028 24th Street • San Francisco, CA 94114
415.643.8877 tel
getupssf@aol.com
Noe Valley

Open

Mon	11:00-7:00
Tues	11:00-7:00
Wed	11:00-7:00
Thurs	11:00-7:00
Fri	11:00-7:00
Sat	10:00-7:00
Sun	11:00-7:00

ANDREA WYNER

Miles

Mellow Noe Valley residents seem to drink a fair amount of coffee, but they got a jolt of another kind with the recent arrival of Miles Barry's new and vintage clothing boutique. Barry left corporate retail to start his own business, where he could indulge in fashion, the ultimate form of self-expression, and encourage his customers to do the same. The name Getups is taken from a poem by Maya Angelou, but that's not his only inspiration. Pop culture relics like Brillo Pad, Tide and Mr. Bubble boxes are backdrops for the funky, edgy mannequin displays—think "Soul Train" meets Andy Warhol. You'll find everything from men's and women's leather coats and glasses to handbags, hats and a fine selection of Levis 501s.

Noe Valley Pet Co.

Pet Store

1451 Church Street • San Francisco, CA 94131
415.282.7385 tel • 415.282.4319 fax
www.noevalleypet.com
Noe Valley

SHARON BEALS

Open

Mon	10:00-8:00
Tues	10:00-8:00
Wed	10:00-8:00
Thurs	10:00-8:00
Fri	10:00-8:00
Sat	10:00-6:00
Sun	10:00-5:00

95

As any pet owner knows, dogs and cats are not just four-legged friends—they're members of the family. And they deserve a store that caters to their doggy and kitty needs. That's where Noe Valley Pet Company comes in. Animal lovers Paula Harris and Celia Sack have a passion for pets—theirs and everyone else's. Why not treat Spike to a plush bed or reward Gracie with catnip fortune cookies? Bring your puppy along on your shopping expedition. Paula and Celia will welcome him with a biscuit. While he's crunching away, stock up on nutritional treats, squishy toys, and other items in this vast pet emporium. You can even pick up something for yourself from among the pet-motif antiques, one of NVPC's specialties.

Paula, Celia & friend

Babette

Women's Apparel

1400 Grant Avenue • San Francisco, CA 94133
28 South Park • San Francisco, CA 94107
415.986.1174 tel (North Beach) • 415.267.0282 tel (SOMA)
www.babettesf.com
North Beach & SOMA

Open: North Beach

Mon	11:00-7:00
Tues	11:00-7:00
Wed	11:00-7:00
Thurs	11:00-7:00
Fri	11:00-7:00
Sat	11:00-6:00
Sun	12:00-5:00

Open: SOMA

Tues	10:00-5:00
Wed	10:00-5:00
Thurs	10:00-5:00
Fri	10:00-5:00
Sat	11:00-5:00

HELGA SIGVALDADÓTTIR

The Babette Collection is all about travel-friendly clothing. Local designer Babette Pinsky combines modern fabrics and sensibilities with fascinating textures and shapes. These easy-to-pack and easy-to-care-for pieces can be worn as daywear or for special evening occasions. The Collection also includes lightweight travel raincoats, lightweight but very warm fleece reversible storm coats and sophisticated soft suiting. The Babette Collection is sold in the Babette stores in North Beach and SOMA, as well as women's boutiques throughout the United States and abroad. The Babette stores also feature accessories and related fashion items from some of her favorite designers.

Babette Pinsky

Conor Fennessy Antiques & Design

Antiques

801 Columbus Avenue • San Francisco, CA 94133
415.673.0277 tel • 415.673.0874 fax
conorfennessy@earthlink.net
North Beach

DAVID LIVINGSTON

Open

Tues	11:00-6:00
Wed	11:00-6:00
Thurs	11:00-6:00
Fri	11:00-6:00
Sat	11:00-6:00
Sun	11:00-6:00

It's the inviting warmth and exuberant style that first draws you into Conor Fennessy Design. But you'll linger in this antiques gallery and design studio and absorb the range of unusual objects and furniture from different times and places. The gallery specializes in unique pieces that can transform your rooms into stylish interiors. From a 19th century Venetian cobalt mirror to a '30s Paul Frankl cocktail table, each object expresses the hand of man through consummate craftsmanship and aesthetic vision. Fennessy is interested in the conversation between objects and their surroundings, and a visit to his gallery is an introduction to the language of interior design. Introductions can lead to great things.

Conor Fennessy

ARCH

Art & Design Supplies

99 Missouri Street • San Francisco, CA 94107
415.433.2724 tel • 415.433.2428 fax
Potrero Hill

Open

Mon	9:00-6:00
Tues	9:00-6:00
Wed	9:00-6:00
Thurs	9:00-6:00
Fri	9:00-6:00
Sat	12:00-5:00

98

SHARON RISEDORPH

Alex, Caryn & Tom

A new addition to Potrero Hill, ARCH is a delightful mix of whimsical tools and serious toys for architects, other design professionals and people who just like art and drafting supplies. It was started over 20 years ago by some architecture school graduates who saw a need and filled it. Its current location is near the cutting-edge California College of Arts & Crafts (CCAC) design school. A lot of experience at listening to the unusual requests of creative individuals and finding ways to address them has generated an eclectic range of merchandise. Whether you're a dyed-in-the-wool luddite still drawing manually, a CAD-proficient techno-geek or merely a design aficionado, ARCH will inspire you to new heights of creative expression or simply encourage you to play.

Grace, Kate, Ruth & Kathy

Friday the Thirteenth West

Art Gallery & Home Furnishings

331 Potrero Avenue • San Francisco, CA 94103
415.863.2285 tel
Potrero Hill

Open
Thurs   1:00-5:00
Fri   1:00-5:00
Sat   1:00-5:00
And by appointment

With "Good Stuff and Art" spelled in vintage lettering over the outside door, you have only a hint of the eccentric mix of art, craft, and iconography within this Portrero Hill storefront. Located in the border territory to the City's artistic South of Market, Mission and Portrero districts, partners Bennie and Suzanne attract an eclectic mix of emerging and established artists, sculptors, and crafts people. They also import a generous dose of exotic art, including what is arguably the Bay Area's best representation of "Outsider Art" from self-taught Alabama artists Jimmy Sudduth and Charlie Lucas. Add to that Mexican wrestling masks, ceramics, furniture and architectural ornaments stacked throughout the front and back rooms and you have the makings of a very interesting afternoon.

Suzanne & Bennie

Good Byes

Consignment Store

3464 Sacramento Street • San Francisco, CA 94110
415.346.6388 tel • 415.674.0150 fax
goodbyes@aol.com
Presidio Heights

Open

Mon	10:00-6:00
Tues	10:00-6:00
Wed	10:00-6:00
Thurs	10:00-8:00
Fri	10:00-6:00
Sat	10:00-6:00
Sun	11:00-5:00

HELGA SIGVALDADOTTIR

Margaret, Pepe, Lynn & Liz

Say hello to Good Byes, "the place where the rich and famous go to unload their clothes." With two stores and countless deals, be prepared to be overwhelmed with temptation at this Presidio Heights consignment shop. Good Byes carries everything from men's and women's formalwear to a wide range of accessories. This is quality thrifting at its best with designers like Prada, Gucci, Chanel, and Armani and labels like Banana Republic and The Gap. You'll find it hard to leave without making a good buy of your own. Just as you suspected, you don't have to be rich and famous to look it.

Thistledown Cottage Gardens

Florist

3695 Sacramento Street • San Francisco, CA 94118
415.346.2555 tel • 415.346.2555 fax
Presidio Heights

Open

Mon	9:00-6:00
Tues	9:00-6:00
Wed	9:00-6:00
Thurs	9:00-6:00
Fri	9:00-6:00
Sat	9:00-6:00

101

HELGA SIGVALDADÓTTIR

Every neighborhood deserves a great flower shop, and Presidio Heights has one. Thistledown Cottage Gardens, tucked along a peaceful residential street, is low-tech and lovely. Owner Rebecca Davidson built up her business through word-of-mouth and stores her customers' names and flower preferences the old-fashioned way—in her head. Open for 13 years, Thistledown specializes in seasonal floral arrangements and stocks an impressive array of orchids. Just tell Rebecca what you're looking for. She and her friendly staff will custom-design a beautiful arrangement of blossoms, herbs, fruit, and branches. Delivery service is available throughout the Bay Area as well as internationally. With one order, you'll be in the "files." Next time around, the folks at Thistledown Cottage Gardens will know who you are.

Travis, Natalie, Rebecca & Alice

Button Down

Men's & Women's Apparel

3415 Sacramento Street • San Francisco, CA 94118
415.563.1311 tel • 415.563.6715 fax
Presidio Heights

Open

Mon	10:00-6:00
Tues	10:00-6:00
Wed	10:00-6:00
Thurs	10:00-6:00
Fri	10:00-6:00
Sat	10:00-6:00

HELGA SIGVALDADÓTTIR

"Luxury doesn't have to shout," says Michael Sabino, owner and founder of Button Down, a high-end men's and women's sportswear specialty store. Located in Presidio Heights, one of San Francisco's grand old neighborhoods, Button Down is a true carriage trade store with a line-up of classic Italian brands, including Etro, Luciano Barbera, Borelli, Avon Celli, Bruli, Allegri, Biella Collezioni, and Longhi. People come in for their weekend togs and take off to Napa Valley, Lake Tahoe, or Pebble Beach. Dressing down is what Button Down is all about; perfect for the professional who dresses down every day.

Michael Sabino

Sue Fisher King

Home Furnishings

3067 Sacramento Street • San Francisco, CA 94115
415.922.7276 tel • 415.922.9241 fax
www.suefisherking.com
Presidio Heights

HELGA SIGVALDADÓTTIR

Open

Mon	10:00-6:00
Tues	10:00-6:00
Wed	10:00-6:00
Thurs	10:00-6:00
Fri	10:00-6:00
Sat	10:00-6:00

Sue Fisher King

For upscale, elegant home furnishings, Sue Fisher King Company is the source. Quality and luxury are the hallmarks of this intimate, inimitable boutique. Since 1979, SFK Co. has specialized in exclusive products from Italy, France, and England. You'll find bed linens, tableware, decorative items, and toiletries you'd ordinarily need a plane ticket to track down. Choose from Italian cashmere throws, Murano chandeliers, French flatware, and English soaps. With what you save in airfare, you can splurge at Sue Fisher King and pamper yourself and your abode with the finest in home accents.

Sarah Shaw

Women's Apparel

3095 Sacramento Street • San Francisco, CA 94115
415.929.2990 tel • 415.929.2989 fax
sshawsf@aol.com
Presidio Heights

Open

Mon	10:00-7:00
Tues	10:00-7:00
Wed	10:00-7:00
Thurs	10:00-7:00
Fri	10:00-7:00
Sat	10:00-7:00
Sun	11:00-5:00

SARAH SHAW COLLECTION

Sarah Shaw

In its three years in Presidio Heights, Sarah Shaw's clothing boutique has put itself on the fashion map. With its high ceilings, chandeliers and fluffy couches, the spacious, sun-drenched shop feels like an elegant sitting room. Shaw carries lines by Trina Turk, Catherine Maladrino, Nanette Lepore, Lilly Pulitzer, and Diane von Furstenberg. Hoping to spread her style outside of her native city, Shaw has just opened a second store on Sonoma Square.

Fetish

Women's Shoes

344 Presidio Avenue • San Francisco, CA 94115
415.409.7429 tel • 415.409.2884 fax
fetishsf@aol.com
Presidio Heights

HELGA SIGVALDADÓTTIR

Open

Mon	10:00-6:00
Tues	10:00-6:00
Wed	10:00-6:00
Thurs	10:00-6:00
Fri	10:00-6:00
Sat	10:00-6:00
Sun	12:00-5:00

105

Few stores can match the fanfare and instant success that welcomed Fetish to Presidio Heights in spring 2000. Fashion Institute graduates Andrea Schnitzer and Sarah Shaw started the shoe salon when they saw a need for a place that would satisfy fashionistas insatiable appetites for the likes of Jimmy Choo, Christian Louboutin, Michel Perry, Jane Brown, and Giuseppe Zanotti. With French antique furnishings, an Italian Murano chandelier overhead, a cool pastel interior contrasting with a rainbow of shoes, and cookies and cappuccino offered up to shoppers, Fetish is thoroughly feminine and utterly irresistible.

Andrea Schnitzer & Sarah Shaw

Brown Eyed Girl

Women's Apparel & Home Furnishings

2999 Washington Street • San Francisco, CA 94115
415.409.0214 tel • 415.409.0215 fax
beg@mindspring.com
Presidio Heights

Open

Mon	11:00-7:00
Tues	11:00-7:00
Wed	11:00-7:00
Thurs	11:00-7:00
Fri	11:00-7:00
Sat	11:00-7:00
Sun	12:00-5:00

HELGA SIGVALDADOTTIR

If Brown Eyed Girl were a political party, pink would be the platform—as in shoes. We're talking fun femininity here: flirty dresses, diamond toe rings, the perfect jeans, soothing bubble bath, plush robes with the store logo (adapted for blue and green eyes, too)—and there are no brown paper bags here; you'll walk away in style with their trademark lingerie bag. Nestled in a converted Victorian, Brown Eyed Girl displays its wares by room—dining room, bath, nursery, and so on. It was all part of creator Danielle Bourhis' grand idea to open a store that celebrated and updated traditional girl turf while paying tribute to the strong connections women share. In that spirit, she joined forces with Tiffany Wendel and the two partners have continued to develop their business with friendship as their bottom line. Come to think of it, Brown Eyed Girl *is* a party, as in slumber, all invited. Get out your pink-foam curlers and go.

Tiffany & Danielle

Mom's the Word

Maternity Wear

3385 Sacramento Street • San Francisco, CA 94118
415.441.8261 tel
www.momstheword.com
Presidio Heights

MOMS THE WORD CO-LECTION

Open

Mon	10:00-6:00
Tues	10:00-6:00
Wed	10:00-6:00
Thurs	10:00-6:00
Fri	10:00-6:00
Sat	10:00-6:00
Sun	12:00-5:00

107

Hajah, Sarah, Alexander & Harrison

Time was when pregnancy meant a good half-year of puffed sleeves, printed smocks, and baggy trousers. Any of these might look fine on a cherub-cheeked infant, but a grown woman? Sarah Pollack conceived the idea of a stylish maternity boutique while she herself was pregnant and Mom's the Word was born. Featuring an impressive selection of clothes for a changing silhouette, Mom's the Word offers mothers-to-be everything from formal eveningwear to comfy jeans, office suiting to lingerie. As any mom knows, becoming a mother doesn't mean a woman stops being all of her other selves—professional, fun, elegant, and yes, sexy. How do you think she got pregnant in the first place?

April in Paris

Custom Leather Work

55 Clement Street • San Francisco, CA 94118
415.750.9910 tel • 415.750.9995 fax
beatrice_amblard@yahoo.com
Richmond

Open

Tues	11:00-5:00
Wed	11:00-5:00
Thurs	11:00-5:00
Fri	11:00-5:00
Sat	11:00-5:00

HELGA SIGVALDADÓTTIR

Beatrice

Simplicity is the guiding principle at April In Paris, a small boutique/workshop where Beatrice Amblard crafts high-quality leather accessories such as handbags, briefcases, wallets, belts, and the ever-popular Palm case. This is the kind of quality workmanship that is meant to be handed down from generation to generation. Bolts of imported leather, crocodile, lizard, ostrich, alligator, and other materials line the shelves. In addition to the selection of ready-made pieces, you can bring in your original ideas, select the color, shape, size, and materials, and Amblard will turn your vision into a unique creation, marked with a signature 18-karat gold bee insignia. Amblard, who came to San Francisco in 1987 after 14 years with the famed house of Hermes, opened her store in spring of 2000.

Satin Moon Fabrics

Fabric Store

32 Clement Street • San Francisco, CA 94118
415.668.1623 tel • 415.668.1623 fax
Richmond

HELGA SIGVALDADÓTTIR

Open

Tues	11:30-6:00
Wed	11:30-6:00
Thurs	11:30-7:00
Fri	11:30-6:00
Sat	11:30-6:00

Alice & Susan

Tucked amidst the neighborly shopping mecca of the Richmond district is Satin Moon Fabrics, a pilgrimage destination in its own right. Owners and sisters Alice and Susan Miyamoto moved to San Francisco 30 years ago for the music and stayed for everything else. Soon after their arrival, they started Satin Moon, where those seeking fashion and design enlightenment can find earthly nirvana in their fine, unusual fabrics and decorative trimmings. Search for inspiration among their quality wares—old world chenilles, damasks, Indian silks, novelty printed/woven fabrics, and rich velvets. You'll leave Satin Moon not only satisfied with their service and selection, but unusually contented with life.

Prize

Home Furnishings

1415 Green Street • San Francisco, CA 94109
415.771.7215 tel
Russian Hill

Open
Wed   11:00-5:30
Thurs   11:00-5:30
Fri   11:00-5:30
Sat   11:00-5:30
Sun   12:00-5:00
And by appointment

CHRISTINA ECKLUND

Jennifer & Christina

The recent burgeoning of business in Russian Hill has rapidly turned it from sleepy neighborhood to destination district. That's why Jennifer Davis and Christina Ecklund decided to open their second Prize store in this up-and-coming area. (The Berkeley store is located at 2361-2363 San Pablo Avenue.) A small but well-stocked gift and vintage home furnishings store, Prize has a distinctly feminine sensibility. But, as its proprietors point out, you never know what to expect—one week, a painted metal apothecary cabinet stuffed with vintage Steiff animals; the next, a French marble bistro table topped with antique cake plates. Prize mainstays include early 20th century furniture, French and Italian chandeliers, English ironstone, hotel silver, 1920s trophies, and schoolhouse maps and globes. If you're looking for a prize, here is where you'll find it.

Smoke Signals

International Newsstand & Smoke Shop

2223 Polk Street • San Francisco, CA 94109
415.292.6025 tel • 415.292.5809 fax
smokesignals@aol.com
Russian Hill

HELGA SIGVALDADÓTTIR

Open

Mon	8:00-8:00
Tues	8:00-8:00
Wed	8:00-8:00
Thurs	8:00-8:00
Fri	8:00-8:00
Sat	8:00-8:00
Sun	8:00-6:00

111

With over 1,500 periodicals from around the world and a wide range of tobacco products, Smoke Signals is the place to stop before ordering your latte. This international newsstand and smoke shop is conveniently nestled amidst a string of cafes and bars in lively Russian Hill. You'll find whole magazine sections devoted to your particular passion or profession—design, architecture, fashion, and technology. Linger over the selection and shoot the breeze with owner Fadi Berbery and his staff in any of the 7 languages they speak collectively. Don't forget to pick up a lotto ticket while you're there. One lucky patron hit the second biggest Lotto jackpot ever—$88 million—with a ticket purchased at Smoke Signals.

Fadi Berbery

Atelier des Modistes

Wedding Gowns & Women's Couture Clothing

1903 Hyde Street • San Francisco, CA 94109
415.775.0545 tel • 415.775.4323 fax
www.atelierdesmodistes.com
Russian Hill

Open

Wed	12:00-8:00
Thurs	12:00-8:00
Fri	12:00-8:00
Sat	12:00-8:00

CHRISTOPHER FARRIS

In Russian Hill, along the tree lined Hyde Street cable car line, you'll find Atelier Des Modistes, the destination for brides-to-be or anyone seeking custom-designed couture and ready-to-wear. Suzanne Hanley is the wellspring behind these creations and she owns the studio with artist Christopher Farris, whose photographs and sculptures grace the gallery-style space. Hanley's designs begin with such luxurious materials as Italian silk satins and shantungs, and beading using precious and semi-precious stones. Each garment is made to complement the personality and taste of the individual, and Hanley's background as a mechanical engineer assures that her finished creations work in symmetry with the body as well as look beautiful. Atelier Des Modistes also offers elegant jewelry to complete your ensemble and unique wedding rings for those who want to declare their union with something other than the traditional gold band.

Christopher, Artemisia & Suzanne

Cris

Consignment Store

2056 Polk Street • San Francisco, CA 94109
415.474.1191 tel • 415.474.2815 fax
Russian Hill

JACOB ZANDER

Open
Mon	11:00-6:30
Tues	11:00-6:30
Wed	11:00-6:30
Thurs	11:00-6:30
Fri	11:00-6:30
Sat	11:00-6:00
Sun	12:00-5:00

113

For 15 years, Cris has catered to women with Champagne taste. The Polk street consignment boutique carries current pret-a-porter styles from Chanel, Prada, Tocca, Hermes, Dolce & Gabbana, Comme des Garçons, as well as American sportswear designers. A native of Milan, fashion is in this former designer's blood. Clothes are always in excellent condition, and some even feature original price tags. A grand mirror and striking displays give Cris an upscale ambience that matches the clothes, as do the solicitous

Cris

SwallowTail

Home Furnishings

2217 Polk Street • San Francisco, CA 94109
415.567.1555 tel • 415.567.1503 fax
Russian Hill

Open

Mon	11:00-6:00
Tues	11:00-6:00
Wed	11:00-6:00
Thurs	11:00-6:00
Fri	11:00-6:00
Sat	11:00-6:00
Sun	11:00-6:00

114

SWALLOWTAIL COLLECTION

Sheri & Kari

Housed in an airy sun-drenched space that resembles a giant greenhouse, SwallowTail achieves its eclectic style thanks to the varied tastes of co-owners Kari Lobdell and Sheri Sheridan. Featuring a sophisticated selection of vintage home decor with a sprinkling of the new, the duo says they are more interested in the look and feel of an object, rather than its brand or provenance. Combing flea markets and estate sales across the country and in Europe to find aesthetically stunning objects from the past 150 years, the pair delights in unexpected arrangements: Turn-of-the-century crystal chandeliers co-exist with industrial steel furniture and 1920s French Nouveau painting. Says Kari, "We enjoy the visual surprises that occur in unconventional juxtapositions."

SFMOMA MuseumStore

Gift Store

151 3rd Street • San Francisco, CA 94103
415.357.4035 tel • 415.357.4043 fax
www.sfmoma.org
SOMA

RICHARD BARNES

Open	
Mon	10:00-6:30
Tues	10:00-6:30
Wed	10:00-6:30
Thurs	10:00-9:00
Fri	10:00-6:30
Sat	10:00-6:30
Sun	10:00-6:30

115

Art and commerce meet at the SFMOMA MuseumStore. Housed on the first floor of the audacious, Botta-designed landmark, the SFMOMA MuseumStore has developed a world-class reputation all its own. Gone are the days when museum stores simply knocked out Tiffany-inspired scarves and replicas of Greek statues. After touring the galleries, you'll find inspired art and design you can take home in the MuseumStore. Check out the impressive selection of art books, the fun and funky logo items, innovative housewares, and jewelry from designers throughout the world. Indulge in guilt-free spending. After all, your purchase helps fund the exhibitions and programming of SFMOMA.

David Ross, Museum Director

ISDA & CO

Men's & Women's Apparel

29 South Park • San Francisco, CA 94107
415.512.1610 tel • 415.512.0315 fax
www.isda-and-co.com
SOMA

Open

Mon	10:00-5:30
Tues	10:00-5:30
Wed	10:00-5:30
Thurs	10:00-5:30
Fri	10:00-5:30
Sat	10:00-5:00

HELGA SIGVALDADÓTTIR

Isda Funari

Women and men all over North America are familiar with ISDA & CO's simple yet stylish fashions, but the heart of the business is the company's San Francisco headquarters. Isda Funari spent 20 years designing for companies like ESPRIT and Union Bay before launching her own business more than a decade ago. Inspired by the Shaker philosophy that something functional can also be beautiful, Funari designs five women's collections and two men's collections a year utilizing cotton, wool, silk, and blends that look as good as they feel. The clean, bright store—a converted warehouse in South Park—also carries her seasonal wardrobe basics, lounge wear, and home accessories.

Limn

Art Gallery, Furniture & Home Furnishings

290 Townsend Street • San Francisco, CA 94107
415.543.5466 tel • 415.543.5971 fax
www.limn.com
SOMA

HELGA SIGVALDADÓTTIR

Open

Mon	9:30-5:30
Tues	9:30-5:30
Wed	9:30-5:30
Thurs	9:30-5:30
Fri	9:30-5:30
Sat	11:00-5:30
Sun	11:00-5:30

117

From its modest beginning as a small North Beach shop catering mainly to design professionals in the early '80s, to its current expansion south of Market, Limn has become synonymous with high design. With 50,000 square feet of gallery space dedicated to fine art, furniture, kitchen, lighting, and home accessories, Limn's SOMA space is nothing short of a temple of modern design. Owner Dan Friedlander describes the business as a place where art and design meet. In addition to the retail store, Limn has an award-winning website (limn.com), and publishers a bi-annual book dedicated to exploring global concepts in design.

Dan Friedlander

**Steve, Bulthaup
Kitchen Manager**

Maison d'Etre

Home Furnishings

92 South Park • San Francisco, CA 94107
415.357.1747 tel • 415.357.1747 fax
www.maisondetre.com
SOMA

Open

Mon	11:00-6:00
Tues	11:00-6:00
Wed	11:00-6:00
Thurs	11:00-6:00
Fri	11:00-6:00
Sat	11:00-5:00

118

FRED WOMAK

Fred & Patty

The name Maison d'Etre suggests this shop's sense of play, elevating home to a new level of passion. An array of eclectic antiques, vintage modern furnishings, unusual home accessories, and whimsical objects all find delightful fusion in this color-bathed space. Located in South Park, rather than the Marais, devotees return regularly to check the latest finds such as oversize metal signage letters, '50s schoolroom globes, French beaded chandeliers—but often end up falling for something quite unexpected. Treasure seekers also discover gorgeous French linens, exquisite champagne flutes, children's games, computer bags, and an assortment of candles. With a combined background in floral and interior design, owners Patty Brunn and Fred Womack have created a store that celebrates the art of living in an aesthetically pleasing environment. True to their motto, their shop will encourage you to, "return to estate of grace."

Ma Maison

Home Furnishings

592 Third Street • San Francisco, CA 94107
415.777.5370 tel • 415.777.2397 fax
www.ma-maison.com
SOMA

HELGA SIGVALDADÓTTIR

Open

Mon	10:00-5:30
Tues	10:00-5:30
Wed	10:00-5:30
Thurs	10:00-5:30
Fri	10:00-5:30
Sat	11:00-5:00

119

Isabelle & John

Francophile Alert: Ma Maison brings Paris to the Bay with a wide range of housewares and home accents from the home of la tour Eiffel. In fact, a mural of the Eiffel Tower overlooks this exquisite selection of Limoges dinnerware, Laguiole cutlery, French linens, pewter serving pieces, Parisian jewelry, and silk scarves, among other items. Husband and wife team John and Isabelle Karatzas started Ma Maison in 1997 after learning firsthand that the Bay Area lacked the sort of specialty home boutiques they frequented in Paris. They shop in France for the beautiful and unique products that the French are so famous for. John and Isabelle will personally guide you through their wares with the attention Europeans are still accustomed to and enable you to bring a taste of France back home.

Cafe Monk

Restaurant

564 Fourth Street • San Francisco, CA 94107
415.777.1331 tel • 415.777.1243 fax
www.cafemonk.com
SOMA

Open

Tues	6:00-10:00
Wed	6:00-10:00
Thurs	6:00-10:00
Fri	6:00-10:00
Sat	6:00-10:00

120

DAVID LIVINGSTON

When Kazuyo and Dan Friedlander began laying the plans for their restaurant, they went to great lengths to ensure that the menu, architecture, and ambiance would relate to the surrounding environment. What they came up with is Cafe Monk, a spacious SOMA restaurant serving Italian-based California cuisine. Chef Randy Windham (of Oliveto's, Liberty Cafe, and Zuni), has created a simple but delectable menu using the choicest ingredients (most of the herbs and vegetables are locally grown, and almost entirely organic). There's no pretense here. Just quality food in a stunning yet understated space. That explains why Cafe Monk attracts such an eclectic crowd of artists, neighbors, and visitors who want to experience quintessential California cuisine. Whether you chose to sit at the 20-person reflectory table for a communal experience, or opt for an intimate booth in the balcony, you'll be surrounded by the restaurant's collection of portraits of famous Monks including Abe Monk, Meredith Monk, Edward Hieronymus Monk, and Thelonious Monk.

Manager Eric Vreede & Chef Randy Windham

Wishbone

Gift Store

601 Irving Street • San Francisco, CA 94122
415.242.5540 tel • 415.242.5541 fax
www.wishbonesf.com
Sunset

HELGA SIGVALDADÓTTIR

Open	
Mon	11:30-7:00
Tues	11:30-7:00
Wed	11:30-7:00
Thurs	11:30-7:00
Fri	11:30-7:00
Sat	11:30-7:00
Sun	11:30-7:00

121

From designer dish racks to sushi print pajamas, Wishbone is a pastiche of modern design and serious whimsy. Started by artists Gay W. Lam and Cory Villano in 1995, the store carries goods that reflect the owners' quirky personal tastes and artistic sensibilities. Its appealing mix of style and humor makes it the ideal spot to shop for fun, affordable items: lunar lunch boxes, sock monkeys, his-and-hers sake cups (mix and match as necessary). Visit Wishbone at the Irving Street location and know the satisfaction of finding the ideal gift, for someone else—or yourself.

Gay, Joseph & Cory

Catherine Jane

Women's Apparel

1234 9th Avenue • San Francisco, CA 94122
415.664.1855 tel • 415.664.5273 fax
www.catherinejane.net
Sunset

Open

Mon	12:00-5:00
Tues	11:00-6:30
Wed	11:00-6:30
Thurs	11:00-6:30
Fri	11:00-6:30
Sat	11:00-6:00
Sun	12:00-5:00

HELGA SIGVALDADÓTTIR

Catherine Jane

Season after season, fabric and silhouettes are the inspiration for Catherine Jane's elegant styles. Take the fog coat, her quintessential layering piece that she makes each year. This time, she used apalca, cashmere, mohair and boiled wool for a sensuous yet practical garment, particularly in the often foggy Inner Sunset, where her small store sits just steps from Golden Gate Park. Lines by Autumn Cashmere, White and Warren, Emozione and Dana Kellin Jewelry and Lisa Nading shoes complement Catherine Jane's chic dresses, skirts, blouses, tunics, and pants and help complete a timeless yet modern look. Personal service and attention to detail are emphasized; customers can make appointments to visit Catherine Jane's back studio and choose from a collection of fabrics and trims for a truly custom look.

First Chop

Women's Apparel

954 Irving Street • San Francisco, CA 94122
415.564.7030 tel
www.firstchopsf.com
Sunset

PEGGY ROVINSKY

Open

Mon	11:00-5:00
Tues	11:00-5:00
Wed	11:00-5:00
Thurs	11:00-5:00
Fri	11:00-5:00

123

Janet Meinsma

A charmed oasis for the collector of fine designer clothing and accessories of recent seasons, First Chop derives its name from a 200-year-old Anglo-Indian expression meaning first in quality, style, or status. When viewing the collection on display, the name says it all. Janet Meinsma, resident "curator" of the collection, considers her store a fashion art gallery with a strict focus on those articles whose design value marks them unmistakably as the collectibles of the future. You'll find everything from one-of-a-kind Italian hill town rings by Vicky Ambery-Smith and custom-designed ivory bangles by Elsa Peretti to deconstructed Comme Des Garçons eveningwear and over-scale Yohji Yamamoto frock coats. First Chop anticipates the future while offering fabulous style right now, giving both customer and designer the royal treatment they so richly deserve.

Pacific Ocean

OCEAN
BEACH

ZOO

GOLDEN GATE
NATIONAL
RECREATION AREA

Blvd.

SUNSET

Sunset Blvd.

Great Highway

Way

CLIFF
HOUSE

Moraga St.

Lincoln

ML King Jr. Dr.

GATE PARK

34th Ave.

LAND'S
END

GOLDEN

JFK Dr.

25th Ave.

Blvd.

Legion of Honor

De Young
Museum

Fulton St.

RICHMOND

SEACLIFF

St.

Balboa St.

Geary

BAKER
BEACH

8th Ave.

Clement St.

Park Presidio

Arguello

California St.

Masonic Ave.

Blvd.

PRESIDIO
HEIGHTS

GOLDEN GATE
NATIONAL
RECREATION
AREA

USF

Geary Blvd.

Presidio Ave.

Arguello

PRESIDIO

Eddy St.

Divisadero

Lyon St

1

Ellis St.

FILLMORE

St.

Blvd.

Doyle Dr.

Laguna

Fillmore

PACIFIC
HEIGHTS

GOLDEN
GATE
BRIDGE

Gough

St.

Pacific St.

Post St.

Franklin

COW
HOLLOW

PALACE OF
FINE ARTS

Van Ness Ave.

St.

Sutter St.

California St.

St.

Union St.

Lombard St.

Marina Blvd.

MARINA GREEN

Bush St.

Pine St.

Sacramento St.

Larkin St.

Broadway

Polk

Van Ness Ave.

MARINA

Clay St.

St.

FORT
MASON

Washington St.

Hyde St.

St.

GRACE
CATHEDRAL

Jackson St.

RUSSIAN
HILL

Leavenworth

North Point St.

AQUATIC
PARK

Pacific

St.

Vallejo

St.

Jones

Beach St.

Green

St.

Jefferson St.

45

Taylor

Columbus Ave.

Bay

Broadway

St.

43

NORTH
BEACH

Mason

FISHERMAN'S
WHARF

41

Union St.

Powell

St.

Filbert St.

Greenwich St.

Stockton

Embarcadero

Pier 39

Lombard St.

St.

Beach St.

TELEGRAPH
HILL

Chestnut St.

Francisco

North Point St.

The

COIT
TOWER

Bay St.

35

N

33

31

29

MAIN LIBRARY

Grove St.
Market St.
Mission St.
7th St.
Howard St.
8th St.
Folsom St.
9th St.
10th St.
Harrison St.
11th St.
12th St.

6th St.
5th St.
Bryant St.
Brannan St.
Townsend St.

SOUTH OF MARKET (SOMA)

4th St.
120
3rd St.
117
PACIFIC BELL PARK

46

San Francisco Bay

48

50

CALTRAIN DEPOT
King St.
Berry St.
Mission Creek Marina

4th St.

52

54

64

80

101

14th St.
15th St.
South Van Ness Ave.
Folsom St.
Harrison St.
16th St.
FRANKLIN SQ.
17th St.
18th St.
19th St.

MISSION

2

Potrero Ave.
99
Division St.
Kansas St.
Rhode Island St.
Carolina St.

16th St.
98
17th St.
JACKSON PLGD.
Mariposa St.
18th St.

POTRERO HILL

6th St.
Missouri St.
Texas St.
Mississippi St.
19th St.
20th St.

3rd St.
Illinois St.
China Basin

68

280

Bryant St.
Hampshire St.
York St.
Florida St.
Alabama St.
20th St.
Treat Ave.
21st St.
22nd St.
23rd St.
Folsom St.
24th St.
Harrison St.
25th St.
Bryant St.
26th St.

SF GENERAL HOSPITAL

Potrero Ave.

Deharo St.
Carolina St.
Wisconsin St.
Arkansas St.

POTRERO HILL REC. CENTER

23rd St.
25th St.

Tennessee St.
Minnesota St.
Indiana St.

22nd St.
3rd St.
24th St.

Cesar Chavez St.

Islais Creek Channel

Mission St.
Cesar Chavez St.
Precita Ave.
PRECITA PK.
Coso Ave.
Peralta Ave.

BERNAL HEIGHTS PARK

Powhattan Ave.

Cortland Ave.

Tompkins Ave.

Bayshore Blvd.

Jerrold Ave.
Evans Ave.
Toland St.

Cargo Way

Evans Ave.
3rd St.
Phelps St.
Industrial St.

280

101

N

.5 MILE

ALPHABETICAL INDEX

CATEGORY INDEX

VINTAGE CLOTHING

WEDDING GOWNS

WOMEN'S APPAREL

WOMEN'S SHOES & ACCESSORIES

Art Director	Dan Easton
Cartographer	Ellen McElhinny
Graphic Design	Mattison Clark
Graphic Design (Cover)	Laurie Frankel
Graphic Design (Logo)	Shawn Hazen
Photographer	Heather de Koning
Photographer	Helga Sigvaldadóttir
Photoshop	Eyeland Media
Printer	SunGold Litho
Scanning	Iris Photo Digital
Writer	Laura Compton
Writer	Roxane Ramos
Web Design	Evolve Design

SPECIAL THANKS TO:

Ronni Daly, Carla Morris, Geoffrey O'Brien, M.B. Nelson, Kari Lobdell, Sheri Sheridan, Brian Flores, Jeoffrey Douglas, Sheila Cohen, Sidney Brown, Autumn Carey-Adamme, Florian Bruins, Don Roberts, Kathryn Yulish, Paul Spiegel, Mike Boerma & Jerry Helmers.

ADDITIONAL PHOTO CREDITS:

Portraits: Helga Sigvaldadóttir: 6-9,12,13,15-18, 21-23, 25-33, 35, 36, 38-45, 47, 49-62, 64-66, 68-81, 83-93, 95-114,116-123; Heather de Koning: 19, 20, 24, 37, 46, 48; Dan Easton 5, 14; Jill Posener 82; Crucita Polizzi 63; Terrance McCarthy 115; Andrea Wyner 94. Cover photo credits, top left to right: Paul Moore, SwallowTail Collection, Richard Barnes, Alison Hoekstra, Helga Sigvaldadóttir, Foreign Cinema Collection, Laurie Frankel. Back cover photo credits: Helga Sigvaldadóttir.

First Edition, 2001

Crown Guides: Unique Places in San Francisco—1st ed.
Includes Index
ISBN 0-9708259-0-0

Every effort has been made to ensure the accuracy of the information in this book. However, certain details are subject to change. The publisher cannot accept responsibility for any consequences arising from the use of this book.

Crown Guides is a publication of Zeitgeist Books
268 Bush Street, No. 2627 San Francisco, California 94104

 Printed on recycled paper